Women and the

Apostolic Ministry?

G. Richmond Bridge

Anglican Chaplain at Dalhousie University and the
University of King's College, and Priest in Charge
of King's College Chapel, Halifax, Nova Scotia

The Convent Society
Halifax

First Published 1997
The Convent Society
Halifax, Nova Scotia
Canada

ISBN 1-895713-10-2

Printed in Canada

To
Captain Patricia Martinson,
stalwart churchman and
sidesman *extraordinaire*

Preface

I wish to thank the Rt. Revd. Robert Mercer, C.R., and the Revd. Canon Dr. Robert D. Crouse, S.S.C., for graciously reading the manuscript and for their valuable advice with this project. I also wish to thank the Rt. Revd. William C. Wantland for his kind assistance in tracking down a reference. I cannot begin to thank the efficient staff of the Library of the University of King's College, Halifax, who have been exceptionally helpful and supportive.

I am indebted to the Very Revd. Br. Francis Charles, O.S.A., Provincial Superior, and the Brethren of the Order of Saint Augustine, and to the Convent Society of the Anglican Catholic Church, for their willingness to publish this work. I owe special thanks to the Revd. Fr. Vincent Anthony, O.S.A., for proof-reading.

Warm words of gratitude and appreciation must be expressed to the Congregation of King's College Chapel, whom I am privileged to serve. Their faithful and cheerful witness inspires and encourages me in all that I undertake.

Finally, I wish to acknowledge the enormous patience shown by Mother Raphael, Dame Philippa, and Dame Constance throughout the writing of this book.

G. Richmond Bridge +

Holy Cross House
Portuguese Cove
26th August, 1997

Contents

Introduction

Still a live issue?

Throughout twenty years of university chaplaincy, one of the questions which students have most often asked is what do I believe about women in the Apostolic Ministry, that is, women as ordained bishops and priests. The frequency with which this question has been asked would indicate that the role of women in the Apostolic Ministry is not the settled or received doctrine that some in the Anglican Church would hope or suggest. Many young, inquiring minds are still grappling with this issue and seeking to understand the reasons for and against ordaining women. I hope that this book will assist them and also others in the exploration for God's unchanging Truth.

I make no pretence that a short book can be an exhaustive theological study of what is a most complex and multifaceted issue. My less ambitious goal is to explain as clearly and simply as possible my own stance, which is to *affirm* the biblical view that the Apostolic Ministry is male. I want to say "yes" to what I believe is the biblical and reasonable Tradition of the Church.

Holy Order

For me, the issue of women in the Apostolic Ministry is fundamentally a matter of order. This should not be surprising in that we speak about the Apostolic Ministry as Holy Orders. The Preface to our Anglican Ordinal begins:

It is evident unto all men diligently reading holy Scripture and ancient Authors that from the Apostles' time there have been these Orders of Ministers in Christ's Church: Bishops, Priests, and Deacons.[1]

[1]*Book of Common Prayer* (Canada, 1959), p. 637. The Italics are mine.

Whose Orders are they? To whom do they belong? The answer for me is, and must be, God. Their divine source and authority explains why these ancient Orders are called *holy:* certainly not because they were devised by humans but because they were given by God, "the giver of all good gifts." Our Prayer-book Collect for Ordinands acknowledges this in praying to God, who of His "divine providence hast appointed divers Orders" in His Church.[1]

Likewise, Richard Hooker (*c.* 1554-1600), Anglican theologian *par excellence*, writes: "The ministry of things divine is a function which as God did himself institute. . . ." Those in Holy Orders, he says, are "ministers of God as from whom their authority is derived, and not from men." Hooker's regard for the ministry is immeasurable:

> The power of the Ministry of God translateth out of darkness into glory; it raiseth men from the earth, and bringeth God himself down from heaven; by blessing visible elements it maketh them invisible grace; it giveth daily the Holy Ghost. . . .

Hooker says that in light of "so great power," we cannot "imagine that any but God can bestow it!"[2] Bishop Jeremy Taylor (1613-1667), another classical Anglican theologian, expresses similar respect for the divine grace of ordination: "The thing is sacred, separate, solemn, deliberate, derivative from God, and not of human provision, or authority, or pretence, or disposition."[3]

Holy Orders, which are "*not* from men," are of God's own plan and making. The blueprint and copyright of Orders are clearly His, and they are found in God's own revelation of Himself, in Holy Scripture.

[1]*Book of Common Prayer* (Canada, 1959), pp. 46, 210, 639, & 646.
[2]Richard Hooker, *Of the Laws of Ecclesiastical Polity*, V.77.1.
[3]Jeremy Taylor, *Of the Office Ministerial,*

1. Holy Scripture

The Order of Creation

As we affirm in the Nicene Creed, Almighty God is the primal source, the "maker of heaven and earth, And of all things visible and invisible."[1] God's creation, both visible and invisible, has a remarkable and coherent order. The Collect for Michaelmas acknowledges that God "hast ordained and constituted the services of Angels and men in a wonderful order. . . ." [2] This order, the first book of the Bible tells us, was most pleasing to its Architect and Builder: "And God saw everything that he had made, and, behold, it was very good" (*Gen.* 1:31).

Genesis also tells us that God's fashioning of the world was anything but a muddle, anything but an arbitrary, haphazard, or disjointed affair. The story of creation, like a well-constructed musical score or literary work, unfolds in a most orderly, intentional manner. From the first through the sixth day, God deliberately and meticulously -- in each and every detail -- wills His creation.

Male and Female

On the sixth day, God creates mankind in His own image, *Imago Dei*. He does not make humanity asexual (without sex) or unisexual (one sex only) or androgynous (hermaphroditic, that is, equally male and female, having both male and female sexual organs), but rather He makes two different sexes: "male and female created He them" (1.27). According to Fr. Charles Caldwell, "We are not like the neuter 'Barbie Doll' of popular culture. We have both belly buttons and genitals, signs that we

---

[1] *Book of Common Prayer*, p. 71.
[2] *Ibid., p. 294.*

11

are from someone and for someone."[1]   In the created order, God's perfect order, humanity is manifested in two distinct genders, which are complementary and interdependent, but distinguishable, not identical, and certainly not interchangeable. For they are too different for that! Dr. Eric Mascall writes: "For the basic fact about the sexes is not that they are inferior or superior to each other but that they are different."[2] This difference is critical to biblical anthropology (the study of mankind).

Any other human distinction, such as race or colour, even circumcision and uncircumcision, is very secondary to this fundamental distinction of male and female sexuality. And, of course, it is impossible to compare God-given, "built-in," distinctions to purely human categories, such as slave or free, which are post-lapsarian ("after the Fall"), man-made differentiations, borne in our sinfulness, things from which we need to be saved. Sexual distinctions are pre-lapsarian ("before the Fall"), part and parcel of the goodness of God's creation.

Fathers and Mothers
Attached to the sexual distinction is the responsibility of procreation: "Be fruitful and multiply, and replenish the earth. . . ." (1:28). Adam and Eve and their descendants are to be procreators, fathers and mothers: "Therefore shall a man leave his father and his mother, and shall cleave unto his wife: and they shall be one flesh" (2:24). A great commentator of the Talmud points out that Adam does not speak here: "These words are by the Holy Spirit."[3] This may explain why this verse from *Genesis* was so important to Jesus, who quotes it in the New Testament.[4]

[1]Charles F. Caldwell, *Head and Glory: Sacred Order or Secular Chaos* (Preservation Press, 1996), p. 62.

[2]E. L. Mascall, *Women Priests?* (Church Literature Association, 1972), p. 11.

[3]Rashi or Rabbi Solomon ben Isaac of Troyes, France (1040-1105), cited by J. H. Hertz, *Genesis*, in *The Pentateuch and Haftorahs* (Oxford University, 1929), p. 24.

[4]*Mt.* 19:4-6, the Gospel appointed for a Nuptial Eucharist in *the Book of Common Prayer* (p. 572). A parallel passage is found in *Mk.* 10:6-9, and St. Paul also cites this passage in *Eph.* 5:31.

The Greek word *(pros)kollao,*[1] translated by the English *cleave* (from the Old English *cleofian*), is graphic; it means "to glue or weld together," "to attach one's self to." *Genesis* is describing not just the physical union but the unique ties, emotional and spiritual, which bind the two different, complementary sexes, which join a man to a woman and make them one entity.

Different sexual anatomy clearly defines the procreative roles: man is to be the father, the seminal force, the progenitor, and the initiator; and woman is to be the receiver. Of course, these sexual differences are not only biological but also have psychological implications and spiritual analogues.[2]

Adam, according to *the Wisdom of Solomon*, is "the first formed father of the world" (10:1). His masculine, paternal role as begetter is not unrelated to God's spiritual, archetypal role as Father in creation and redemption. God takes the initiative: He makes and saves and justifies. God, the Eternal Begetter, always inaugurates; in the lovely phrase of Gerard Manley Hopkins, "He fathers-forth whose beauty is past change."[3] God's fatherhood, as well as Adam's, are not fiction; they are God's own revelation. St. Paul writes: "I bow my knees unto the Father [Gk. *pater*]. . . of whom the whole family [*patria,* from *pater*] in heaven and earth is named"(*Eph.*3:14-15). St. Athanasias (*c.* 296-373) wrote that "he who calls God Father, names him from the Word."[4] As unpalatable as this paternity

[1]This word is also used by the *Septuagint* (the Greek translation of the Hebrew Bible), in *Genesis* 2:24.

[2]An excellent summary of the physical, psychological, and spiritual differences between men and women is found in Manfred Hauke, *Women in the Priesthood? A Systematic Analysis in the Light of the Order of Creation and Redemption,* trans. David Kipp (San Francisco, 1988), pp. 85-120. This work by Dr. Hauke, a Professor at the University of Augsburg, is considered a standard reference on the subject.

[3]G. M. Hopkins, "Pied Beauty" (1877), line 10.

[4]Athanasius, *contra Arianos,* I.60. St. Athanasius is speaking against the Arian heretics in the fourth century, who called God *agennetos* ("unoriginate") so as to avoid the personal term "Father" as well as any notion of a Son. St. Athanasius points out that it is Christ's will that the Church baptizes "not into the Name of the Unoriginate and originate, nor into the Name of the Creator

may be to contemporary feminist theologians, who wish to move beyond masculine imagery for the Deity, this is God's revelation of Himself in Scripture, and is not optional or disposable imagery.[1]

The Priority of Adam

In the second creation narrative in *Genesis*, we are informed that God does not want Adam to be alone but creates a "help meet" (helpmate) for him (2:18), someone to be at his side, someone in fact made from Adam's side, from Adam's rib (2:21-22). Eve is bone of Adam's bones and flesh of his flesh (2:23). We need not get too caught up in the intricacies of this mythological surgery to grasp the fundamental point. In the order of creation, man came first and then woman, Adam's "help meet." The word "woman" literally translates "from man"; as Genesis explains, "she was taken out of man" (2:23). In the Hebrew there appears to be a play on words: Woman, *'ischscha* (literally "female man"), is taken out of man, *'isch*. Adam, then, is representative of both sexes in a way that Eve cannot be.

This priority of the male gender is very significant to St. Paul, who writes: "For the man is not of the woman; but the woman of the man" (*1 Cor.* 11:8). Again, the Apostle writes: "For Adam was first formed, then Eve" (*1 Tim* 2:13). This order does not suggest that man is superior or better than woman, or even stronger, for God saw that "every thing that He had made" was "very good" (1:31). St. Ambrose (*c.* 339-97), Bishop of Milan, points out that God called His creation "very good" only after He created woman: "When Adam alone was created, it was not said that it was good."[2] St. Paul had already emphasized the complete

and creature, but into the Name of the Father, the Son, and the Holy Ghost." A generation later, Bishop Severian (*c.* 400) wrote: "The name of 'Father' has not gone up from us, but has come to us from above; for it is manifest that God is Father by nature and not only in name." Cited in J. Armitage Robinson, *St. Paul's Epistle to the Ephesians* (Macmillan, 1903), p. 174.

[1]Typical of many feminist theologians is Mary Daly, who has written an influential book entitled *Beyond God the Father: towards a philosophy of Women's Liberation* (The Woman's Press, 1973).

[2]Ambrose, *De Paradiso*, 10.47.

interdependence of the two sexes: "Nevertheless neither is the man without the woman, neither the woman without the man, in the Lord. For as the woman is of the man, even so is the man also by the woman; but all things of God" (*1 Cor.* 11:11-12).

Notwithstanding, there still is a God-given, God-devised, order and plan: man, "the image and glory of God" (*1 Cor.* 11:7), was created first, then woman, "the glory of the man," as a helpmate. The priority of man is not male chauvinism or patriarchal insensitivity, but simply the biblical and truthful revelation of God's own order.[1] Fr. Michael Harper argues that this biblical view of man and woman is consonant with the laws of nature; it belongs to the same kind of fundamental truth as "Dogs have four legs."[2] General Synods can assert that dogs have five legs, but that assertion does not alter the testimony of nature that dogs have four legs. Synod can say that the sexes are interchangeable and that women can be fathers and priests, but that does not change God's order revealed in Scripture.

The Order of Redemption
The New Testament reveals that Jesus Christ, the Incarnate Word, is the "firstborn of every creature" (*Col.* 1:15), the "firstfruits of his creatures" (*Jas. 1:18*). In Him, all of creation is redeemed and divine order restored. The particularities of creation, including the significant distinctions of human maleness and femaleness, are not obliterated or even blurred. We are saved human beings, but also saved men and saved women. Sexual distinctions are fulfilled in Christ, accentuated and affirmed, and indeed they form a significant part of salvation

[1]Dr. Roger Beckwith, of Latimer House, Oxford, has written a concise and thoughtful essay on the pertinent biblical theology: "The Bearing of Holy Scripture," in *Man, Woman, & Priesthood*, ed. Peter Moore (SPCK, 1978), pp. 45-62. A German systematic theologian, Werner Neuer, from Tübingen, has also published a book on this subject: *Man and Woman in Christian Perspective*, trans. Gordon Wenham (Hodder & Stoughton, 1990).

[2]Michael Harper, *Equal and Different: Male and Female in Church and Family* (Hodder & Stoughton, 1994), pp. 1-2. Fr. Harper, who was a leader in the Anglican charismatic movement and author of several books on the subject, has recently become an Orthodox priest.

15

history. St. Thomas Aquinas (*c.* 1225-74) has taught: "Grace does not destroy nature but completes it."[1]

The New Covenant in Christ does not repudiate the Old; it does not overturn the *Genesis* account of creation. As Article VII puts it,

> The Old Testament is not contrary to the New: for both in the Old and New Testament everlasting life is offered to Mankind by Christ, who is the only Mediator between God and Man, being both God and Man.[2]

Jesus as a Male

Christ, bone of our bones and flesh of our flesh, is, according to St. Paul, "the last Adam" (*1 Cor.* 15:45), not the last Eve! He is the fulfilment of the Old Testament prophecies that a male Messiah or King would save His people. Of course, Jesus came to redeem all of creation, including the entire human race, men and women, both of whom, says Scripture, are contained in man. Yet our Lord's universal mission does not in any way cancel out the particularity of His own Incarnation. His generic humanity, as important as that is, does not eradicate the particularity of His masculinity. Again and again, Scripture tells us that God works through the particular and specific to the universal.

God could easily have been incarnate as a woman or an androgynous being, but He was incarnate as a man -- not through the toss of a coin, but through a deliberate, purposeful choice by "the only wise God" (*1 Tim.*1:17 & *Jude* 25). As Dr. Manfred Hauke puts it, "God does not play dice."[3] We should not try to second-guess God in these matters. Nevertheless, some speculate that God would probably have come as a woman or hermaphrodite in our century. Some speculate that He had no choice but to come as a man in first-century, patriarchal Palestine. Such speculation goes nowhere; one merely replaces cultural norms and assumptions of first-century Palestine with

[1]Thomas Aquinas, *Summa Theologia*, I a, q. 1, a. 8, *ad* 2.
[2]*Book of Common Prayer*, p. 701.
[3]M. Hauke, *Women in the Priesthood?*, p. 230

16

those of late twentieth-century western society. We need to look beyond cultural and temporal arguments to God's eternal will.

Whatever one may conjecture, God chose the perfect moment in history. St. Paul says that "when the fullness of the time was come" -- that is, at the precise time and in the precise place and culture which God chose -- "God sent forth his Son, made of a woman, made under the law" (*Gal.* 4:4). The Incarnation, an unprecedented and unparalleled moment, is the definitive, historical moment that God became man; in the words of T. S. Eliot (1888-1965), it is "the point of intersection of the timeless / With time."[1] No twentieth-century cultural theories, time frames, or personal prejudices can possibly minimize that divine, stupendous, one-moment event.

To the disappointment of many, God's choice of venue for the Incarnation was not twentieth-century London, New York, or Toronto, but first-century Palestine. We may not like some of the other details of His Incarnate Life, like the fact that Jesus was born in Bethlehem, or grew up in Nazareth, the son of a carpenter. But all these details, all these particularities, were God's choice, not ours, and are part of the biblical and historical record. We must acknowledge that God has made decisions. It is presumptuous to think otherwise. The title of a recent book on inclusive language says it all: *Let God be God;*[2] let Him make His own decisions.

God, in His infinite wisdom, chose the details of the Incarnation, which was no dream or surreal exercise, but an actual, historical event. Dr. J. I. Packer writes of the historical reality of the Incarnation in these terms:

> Jesus is the second man, the last Adam, our great high priest and sacrifice, our prophet, priest, and king (not prophetess, priestess,

[1] T. S. Eliot, *Dry Salvages,* V, lines 201-2.

[2] Graham Leonard, Iain MacKenzie, & Peter Toon, *Let God be God* (Dartman, Longman and Todd, 1989). This book is a refutation of feminist, inclusive language liturgies unfaithful to divine revelation. The authors write: "We wish to show that Father is the name by which God both chose and chooses to be known. It is God's self-naming, and this we cannot ignore" (p. 48).

and queen), and he is all this precisely in his maleness. To minimize the maleness shows a degree of failure to grasp the space-time reality and redemptive significance of the incarnation.[1]

Jesus, who was born a male also died as a male on the cross. Edwina Sandys' infamous crucifix, depicting the Christ figure as a female, may be imaginative, but most definitely it is not historically or theologically accurate. Jesus the man, not the woman, died on the cross for the sins of all mankind, for all men and all women. To gloss over the maleness of Christ as though it were unimportant and that only his humanity mattered is to flirt with Docetism, one of the early heresies. Docetism (from Gk. *dokéo* = "seem") taught that Christ only appeared, only seemed to be a man; His appearances were phantasmal, not real; even His suffering on the cross was not real. Against such teaching, Fr. John Saward splendidly summarizes the orthodox understanding of our Lord's sacrificial and life-giving death as a real man:

> His crucified body is creative and generative: in his flesh he has created a new humanity (*Eph.* 2.15ff); by the offering of his body we have been sanctified (*Heb.* 10.10), not some characterless, generalized, docetic body, but his very body, his male body.[2]

Jesus and His Father

Jesus is the Son, not the daughter, of the Living God. He is God's perfect revelation of Himself, "the image of the invisible God" (*Col.* 1:5) and "the express image of His person" (*Heb.* 1:3). Jesus says, "I and my Father are one" (*Jn.* 10:30); and again, "He that hath seen me hath seen the Father" (*Jn.* 14:9).

[1]J. I. Packer, "Introduction," in *Man, Woman & Priesthood,* ed. James Tolhurst (Gracewing, 1989), p. xiii. It should be noted that there are two books, both collections of essays, with the same title, except for a comma. *Man, Woman, & Priesthood* (1978), cited on p. 8, footnote 2, is edited by Peter Moore, former Dean of St. Alban's Abbey. This footnote refers to a later book (1989), edited by J. Tolhurst.

[2]John Saward, *Christ and his Bride* (Church Literature Association, 1977), p. 8. This is a perceptive and helpful tract.

18

Jesus had to represent the fatherhood of God; He had to speak with the likeness and authority of the Father, the King and Lord of Israel, the Divine Master and Judge.

God who is beyond all human categories, who is "without body, parts, or passions,"[1] has not left us to arbitrary, permissive images about Himself. He has chosen to make Himself known to us through the natural world and its specific order. In the pages of Scripture, He has revealed Himself as Father and taught us to call Him Father. Jesus calls Him "Abba" or "Daddy" (*Mk.* 14:36) and teaches the whole Church to pray "Our Father" (*Mt.* 6:9).[2] Christ's understanding of God as Father is extremely well documented. Dr. William Oddie points out that in the New Testament the term "Father" is used at least 170 times by Christ Himself.[3] Dr. Oddie writes:

> For at no point does Jesus imply that God is merely *like* a father to him: his message is that in very truth *God actually is his father*. He is begotten, not made. And this understanding is at the heart of the faith of the early Church.[4]

In order to be the perfect image of the Father, Christ had to be male. If this is "patriarchal," then it is God's patriarchy and, therefore, cannot be anything but wholesome and good.[5] "For thy judgements are good," says the Psalmist (119:39).

The Order of Christ's Church

Jesus Christ, the Second Adam, orders His church as intentionally as God the Father ordered the created world. St. Clement (*fl. c.* 96), Bishop of Rome, tells the Corinthians:

[1] Article I, *Book of Common Prayer*, p. 699.

[2] Literature of the Gnostic heresy abounds with references to God as Mother. In the *Gospel to the Hebrews*, Jesus refers to "My Mother, the Spirit." There are also many androgynous references to God as a great male-female power.

[3] William Oddie, *What will Happen to God? Feminism and the Reconstruction of Christian Belief* (SPCK, 1984), p. 104.

[4] *Ibid.*, p. 119.

[5] For a very positive and sensible evaluation of patriarchy, see Peter Toon, *Let Women be Women* (Gracewing, 1990), pp. 82-86. Dr. Toon concludes that "patriarchy is still viable within family and church today, and, moreover, is the will of God" (p. 86).

19

"Christ therefore is from God, and the Apostles are from Christ; in both cases all was done in good order according to God's will."[1]   The Church and her ministry are God's order, His creation. To repeat Hooker's words, "The ministry of things divine is a function which as God did himself institute. . . ."[2]

Jesus organizes His Church as the new Israel and calls and appoints twelve Apostles (*Mt.* 10:1-5; *Mk.* 3:14-19; *Lk.* 6:13-16), just as God had called the Hebrews to set aside their priesthood in Aaron and the House of Levi: "And no man taketh this honour unto himself, but he that is called of God, as was Aaron" (*Heb.* 5:4).   Our Lord's specific appointment of Twelve, of course,   recalls   the   twelve   tribes   of   Israel   and   God's commanding Moses to appoint their heads (*Num.*1:4-16). Likewise, the Church's Apostles are appointed "a kingdom" by Jesus, and He tells them that they "shall sit on thrones, judging the twelve tribes of Israel" (*Lk.* 22:29-30).

The Apostles are to be the foundation stones of our Saviour's new creation, Christ Himself being the chief cornerstone, the one Lord, "by whom are all things" (*1 Cor.* 8:6).   The Apostles are to represent Christ, the true Apostle of the Father, to the world: "He that receiveth you receiveth me, and he that receiveth me receiveth him that sent me" (*Mt.* 10:40). He instructs them in the Faith and commands them to teach and baptize (*Mt.* 28:19). He gives them authority over unclean spirits and sends them out to preach and heal (*Mt.* 10:1; *Mk.* 6:7; *Lk.* 9:1-2). At the feeding of the multitude, He has them administer in His name (*Mt.* 14:19; *Mk.* 8:6; *Lk. 9:16; Jn.* 6:11). At the Last Supper, he commands them to "do this in remembrance of me" (*Lk.*   22:19; *1 Cor.* 11:25),   that is, to preside in His place at the Eucharist.   On Easter, he breathes upon them and gives them authority to remit and retain sins (*Jn.* 20:22-23); and on Pentecost, He sends the life-giving, invigorating Spirit upon them (*Acts* 2:1-11).

[1]*The First Epistle of Clement to the Corinthians*, 42.2., trans. W. K. Lowther Clarke (1937). James A. Kleist translates the second clause: "Both these orderly arrangements, therefore, originate from the will of God" (1946).
[2]Richard Hooker, *Of the Laws of Ecclesiastical Polity*, V.77.1

There is nothing accidental or capricious in our Lord's choosing and subsequently equipping the Twelve. His is a most deliberate and careful choice, made in obedience to the Father's will. "As the Father gave me commandment, even so I do," says Jesus (*Jn.* 14:31; see also 8:28-29). St. Luke tells us that the Twelve are chosen after Christ had spent an entire night in prayer (*Lk.* 6:12). Our Lord's deliberateness is echoed in His words to Simon Peter: "Upon this rock, I will build *my* church" (*Mt.* 16:18). Elsewhere, and just as deliberately, He tells the Twelve: "Ye have not chosen me, but I have chosen you, and ordained you" (*Jn.* 15:16). Likewise, He says, "As my Father hath sent me, even so send I you" (*Jn.* 20:21). *Acts* refers to the Apostles as those "whom he [Christ] had chosen" (*Acts* 1.2). Bishop Robert Terwilliger (1917-1991) truthfully summed up our Lord's choosing of the Twelve: "If ever he did a deliberate deed, it was this deed."[1] Whatever discrimination there is in this choosing and appointing, it is divine discrimination and most intentional.

Twelve Male Apostles

The twelve chosen and appointed Apostles were all males,[2] just as the priests of Israel were all males. Recall for a moment the various pictures or depictions of Christ and his male Apostles you may have seen. The cover picture on this booklet, from a twelfth-century French illumination, *a Vita Christi*, shows Christ washing the Apostles' feet. One may be more familiar with depictions of the Last Supper: our Lord and His twelve male Apostles gathered around the table. This is not a matter of artistic license but is an historical event, recorded in Scripture: "Now when even was come, he sat down with the twelve" (*Mt.* 26:20;

[1]Robert E. Terwilliger, *Ordination of Men in Theological Perspective* (Forward Movement Publications, n.d.), p. 18.

[2]The reference to Junia as an apostle in *Romans* 16:7 should not confuse us. The notion of a woman apostle, which some feminist theologians have championed, is totally incompatible with the teachings of St. Paul. Some scholars believe that the reference to *Juonias* is an abbreviated form of *Jounianos*, a masculine name. On the other hand, it could simply place a woman named Junia in the wider, lay apostolate, which all Christians share. All Christians are called and sent by Christ, but not all are given Apostolic Orders.

see also *Mk.* 14:17-18 and *Lk.* 22:14).

If one accepts the time frame of the Synoptic Gospels (*Mt.*, *Mk.*, & *Lk.*) and holds that the Last Supper was a Passover Meal, it is remarkable that Christ sat down with the Twelve. For Passover was a family affair, with women and children present. It is as though Christ were intent on making His point about the male Apostles, those to whom He gave authority to celebrate the Eucharist: "Do this in remembrance of me" (*Lk.* 22:19; *1 Cor.* 11:25). The Greek word used by both St. Luke and St. Paul for "remembrance" is *anamnesis*. The Apostles and their successors are to celebrate the Eucharist as an *anamnesis:* as a "memorial," a "reminder," a "commemoration," a "recollection," a "recalling," a "making present," a "re-presentation," of Christ. It is only sensible -- and should be obvious to anyone -- that in this Eucharistic "re-presentation," the Apostolic Minister who presides in the place of Christ is a male. In another chapter, I shall say more about this symbolic standing in the place of Christ and speaking in the person of Christ.

In any case, our Lord's choosing of twelve men was no mistake, for God in Christ, "the giver of every good gift," would not have given an imperfect, incomplete, or unwhole gift to His beloved Church.

Christ and His Mother
Christ could have included women in his Apostolic band. He was, after all, no misogynist (woman-hater). He was a man born of woman -- and a most extraordinary woman, whom He dearly loved and honoured and cared for, even from the cross (*Jn.* 19:26-7).

The Blessed Virgin Mary was specifically chosen by God and called by Him to be the Mother of Jesus, the new Eve. She obediently answered the call, submitting herself to God and fully co-operating with Him: "Behold the handmaid of the Lord; be it unto me according to thy word" (*Lk.* 1:38). With that acceptance, that devout receiving of the Word, she becomes the

Mother of God, whom the Council of Ephesus (431 A.D.) named *Theotokos* (God-bearer) -- a most extraordinary vocation! Both St. Gabriel and St. Elizabeth recognized Mary's unique role in salvation history: "Hail, thou that art highly favoured" (*Lk.* 1:28); "Blessed are thou among women" (42). Likewise, the woman in a crowd spoke a great truth: "Blessed is the womb that bare thee, and the paps which thou hast sucked" (*Lk.* 11:27). In spite of all this, Jesus did not invite His Mother to sit with the Twelve Apostles on the first Maundy Thursday or to be numbered among them.

Other Women

One of the most important of our Lord's recorded conversations was with a Samaritan woman by a well (*Jn.* 4:6-30), even though his disciples "marvelled that he talked with the woman" (4:27). Who could forget His words to the woman taken in adultery (*Jn* 8:4-11)? He encouraged Mary, the sister of Martha, to sit at His feet as a disciple (*Lk.* 10:38-42). It is obvious that our Lord was no male chauvinist. He thoroughly enjoyed talking with women, and He took them seriously -- something that was not the general practice of His day. He healed a woman who was suffering from hemorrhages and who, by Jewish Law, would have been unclean and untouchable (*Mt.* 9:20-22). He affirms the equality of women in marriage (*Mk.* 10:2-12; *Mt.* 19:3-9). He let another woman anoint Him with oil, and called her ministration "a beautiful thing" (*Mt.* 26:7; *Mk.* 14:3; *Lk.* 7:44-48). From the beginning of His ministry, He was surrounded by a faithful band of women (*Lk.* 8:2-3), who even followed Him to the cross (*Lk.* 23:27-28 & 49), stood under it (*Jn.* 19:25), and sought to care for His lifeless body (*Mk.* 16.1; *Lk.* 23:55ff). Risen from the tomb, He first appeared to women (*Mt.* 28:9), especially to St. Mary Magdalene (*Jn* 20:14-18; *Mk.* 16:9). Women, not men, were the first chosen to see His Risen Body; women were commissioned to go and tell the Twelve Apostles.

Given His very positive and remarkably "progressive" views about women, our Lord could easily be thought of as a "feminist."[1] It would, therefore, have been quite natural for Him to have called women to His Apostolic ministry, but He did not. Women are conspicuously absent from the scriptural lists of the Twelve, from both the Last Supper and the Descent of the Spirit on Pentecost.

The Swiss Reformed theologian, Professor Jean-Jacques von Allmen, has written:

> To no woman does Jesus say, "He who hears you, hears me." To no woman does He make the promise to ratify in heaven what she has bound or loosed on earth. To no woman does He entrust the ministry of public preaching. To no woman does He give the command to baptize or to preside at the communion of His Body and Blood. To no woman does He commit His flock.[2]

A Culturally-Controlled Christ?

Arguments that God in Christ was culturally-conditioned, constrained by a specific culture or time to be born as a man and to call only male Apostles as His successors, are not convincing. First of all, the Incarnation, as Dr. Edward Norman argues in the 1978 Reith Lectures, "is the one event in history that stands outside the cultural values of men." Christians, according to Dr. Norman, cannot rely only on "the idealism of men" but must see "the Christ who claimed that he was before Abraham, and who is forever reminding men that heaven and earth shall pass away."[3] Jesus Christ, "God, of God; Light, of Light, Very God, of very God,"[4] cannot be contained by arguments of cultural relativism.

Moreover, it must be pointed out that the culture of our Lord's day was not unfriendly to women religious leaders. Vestal

[1]Fr. Michael Harper points out that Jesus "was not introducing a new feminist gospel. He was simply restoring the sexual equality stated in Genesis 1." *Equal and Different*, p. 41

[2]Jean-Jacques von Allmen, "Is the Ordination of Women to the Pastoral Ministry Justifiable?" in *Sexuality - Theology - Priesthood*, ed. H. Karl Lutge (Concerned Fellow Episcopalians, n.d.), p. 35.

[3]Edward Norman, *Christianity and the World Order* (Oxford University Press, 1979), p. 83.

[4]Nicene Creed, *Book of Common Prayer*, p. 71.

virgins, priestesses, sibyls, prophetesses, and other women religious figures were commonplace in the Mediterranean world of our Lord's ministry, not to mention women teachers of philosophy. Even if this had not been the case, Christ Himself was known to have taken radical or revolutionary steps and to have broken time-honoured rules and customs: healing on the Sabbath, eating with publicans and sinners, discussing religion with women, calling a tax-collector as an Apostle. This most unusual and untypical King, who was born in a stable, rode a donkey, and was crucified with malefactors, overturned more than the tables of the money-changers: "Ye have heard that it was said by them of old time. . . But I say unto you. . . ." (*Mt.* 5:21-22; 27-28; 33-34).

Obviously more than deference to His culture and its customs caused our Lord to choose only male Apostles. Surely the Eternal Christ, who was without sin, who broke the bonds of death forever, could not be inhibited, held captive, by mere social customs and cultural norms of His day. "Even his enemies," writes Dr. Eric Mascall, never accused him of conventionality or cowardice, and it would ill become his disciples in the twentieth century to do so."[1]

The scriptural record cannot be explained away or dismissed. It is clear and unambiguous: Jesus Christ chose twelve men to be His Apostles and gave them authority to carry on His work, to witness to Him, to represent Him in the teaching, sacramental, and pastoral offices. This is clearly what He did, not out of ignorance, cultural bias, or in error. As Pope Paul VI once said, "We cannot change what our Lord did . . . ."[2]

What Jesus did must be important to His Church, as important as what He said. There is in His divine life a perfect harmony

---

[1]E. L. Mascall, "Women and the Priesthood of the Church," in *Why not? Priesthood & the Ministry of Women*, ed. M. Bruce & C. E. Duffield (Marcham, 1972), p. 102.

[2]*Acta Apostolicae Sedis*, 67 (1975), p. 265. In this speech, His Holiness makes it perfectly clear that although our Lord did not call women to "the ordained ministries," He did call women "as disciples and co-workers."

between word and action, between saying and doing. What Jesus did or did not do, like what He said or did not say, must be vitally significant to us who seek to follow Him. We dare not forget that He is Lord of His Church, the chief "Shepherd and Bishop" of our souls (*1 Pt.* 2:25) and "the Apostle and High Priest of our profession" (*Heb.* 3:1)"; and that His will for His church is far more significant than ours. Bishop Kallistos Ware asks a most pertinent question: "Are we to assert that the Incarnate Word and Wisdom of God was mistaken, and that we at the end of the twentieth century understand the truth better than he did?"[1]

The Apostolic Church

After our Lord's death and resurrection, the Apostolic Church which He had established continued to honour and obey her Founder's example in appointing only males to the Apostolic Ministry. St. Matthias, a male Apostle, was chosen to succeed Judas. Despite the availability of many faithful women, only men were considered: "Wherefore of these men. . ." (*Acts* 1:20-24). Bishop Jeremy Taylor (1613-67), calls the Apostles "a spiritual paternity," who "begat the family by the power of the Word and the life of the Spirit, and they fed the family, and ruled it. . . ."[2]

To assist with the ministry, the Apostles appointed deacons (*Acts* 6:1-4) and bishops (presbyters or elders). St. Clement confirms that the Apostles appointed their successors "to act as bishops and deacons for future generations of believers."[3] Hence, there existed in the New Testament Church, three distinct orders of ministry: Apostles (later to be bishops), presbyters/bishops (later to be priests), and deacons. This pattern, of course, parallels the Old Testament ministry of High Priest, Priest, and

---

[1]Kallistos Ware, "Man, Woman, and the Priesthood of Christ," in *Man, Woman, & Priesthood*, ed. Peter Moore (SPCK, 1978), p. 73. This article also appears in *Women and the Priesthood*, ed. Thomas Hopko (St. Vladimir's, 1983), pp. 9-37.
[2]Jeremy Taylor, "A Consecration Sermon, preached at Dublin" (*Lk.* 12:42-43).
[3]Clement of Rome, *1 Cor.* 42:4.

Levite. And just as the Old Testament ministry was restricted to males, so was that of the New Testament. The New Covenant was a fulfilment, not an abolition, of the law.

If Gentiles, Why Not Women?

The same Apostolic Church decided that circumcision was not binding on Christians and that Gentiles could be admitted to the Church (*Acts* 15). We know that Gentiles like St. Timothy (*Acts* 16:3) and St. Titus (*Gal.* 2:3) held Apostolic office in the New Testament Church.[1] However, this same Church gave no Apostolic authority for admitting women to Holy Orders. What the Apostles did or did not do, like what our Lord did or did not do, must be important to us who claim, in the words of the Nicene Creed, to belong to the "Catholic, and Apostolic Church."[2]

In both instances -- ordaining Gentiles and not ordaining women -- the Apostles surely were not operating on their own authority, but on that of Christ, who had patiently instructed them and who had promised that the Holy Spirit would remind them of His teachings (*Jn.* 14:26) and guide them into all truth (*Jn.* 16:13). Obviously the Apostles did not see the decision to ordain Gentile men as being incompatible with our Lord's teachings, including His great missionary commandment (*Mt.*28:19) and the universal implications of His own apostolate (*Jn.*12:32). It must also be emphasized that the decision to admit Gentiles to the Apostolic Ministry was made by the Apostles themselves, eyewitnesses to the Christ, and not by us almost 2,000 years later.

Role of Women in the New Testament

Propriety demanded that there be deaconesses to assist with the baptism and anointing of women candidates. But far beyond this minor liturgical functioning, women had generally prominent and influential roles in the Apostolic Church. Women were

[1]The Calendar in the Canadian Prayerbook refers to St. Timothy and St. Titus as "Apostolic men" (p. ix).

[2]*Book of Common Prayer*, p. 72.

27

greatly involved in the lay apostolate, which is not the same as the ordained Apostolic Ministry of the Twelve. For example, the Jerusalem Church met in the house of Mary (*Acts* 12;12); other significant Christian women included Lydia (*Acts* 16:14), Prisca or Priscilla (*Acts* 18:2), Chloe (*1 Cor.* 1:121), and Phoebe (*Rom.* 16:1).[1]   Many women of the New Testament Church, including the daughters of Philip of Caesarea (*Acts* 21:9), were prophetesses, as were Old Covenant women like Miriam and Deborah and also Anna, who attended our Lord's presentation in the temple (*Lk.* 2:36).[2] It must be noted that prophesying was an individual, spiritual gift, and not a teaching, Apostolic office.[3] In neither the Old Testament nor the New, in neither the old Israel nor the new, did women occupy a teaching or priestly office.

The Apostolic Witness

That the Apostolic Ministry had to be male was very much a part of the New Testament Church's conscious understanding, of her having "the mind of Christ" (*1 Cor.* 2:16), and is amply reflected in the Pauline epistles. A Church which professes to be Apostolic and to have the Apostolic Ministry cannot with any credibility divorce herself from the Apostles' teaching and practice. She cannot reject the Apostolic Tradition and still claim the title, *Apostolic*. Ministers of Christ, says St. Paul, must be accountable, must be "stewards [keepers] of the mysteries of God" and "found faithful" (*1 Cor.* 4:1-2).

[1] Although Phoebe is referred to as a deacon, this may be a grammatical error, or her diaconate is to be taken in the general sense of "servant." There is no evidence that she or any other woman functioned liturgically as a deacon at the Eucharist.

[2] A reference to Deborah raises the question of why women like her are allowed to govern in the Bible. St. Thomas Aquinas (*c.* 1225-74) points out that Deborah "exercised authority in temporal, not in priestly matters." (*Summa Theologica*, III, q. 38, a. 1). John Calvin (1509-64) writes of Deborah's rule: "God's extraordinary acts do not annul the ordinary rules by which He wishes to be bound" (*Commentary, 1 Tim. 2:12*).

[3] St. Thomas Aquinas explains that "Prophecy is not a sacrament but a gift of God." Women "can receive the gift of prophecy and the like, but not the sacrament of Orders" (*Summa Theologica*, III, q. 38. a. 1.).

In the second part of the Prayer-book Catechism, the catechist asks why the Church is called Apostolic. The answer is: "Because it received its divine mission from Christ through his Apostles, and *continues* in their doctrine and fellowship."[1] St. Irenaeus (*c.* 130-200), Bishop of Lyons, said that the Apostles,

like a rich man depositing his money in a bank, delivered into her [the Church's] hands in the fullest measure the whole truth: so that every man, whosoever will, can draw from her the water of life. For she is the entrance to life; all others are thieves and robbers.[2]

The Apostolic deposit, the Apostolic beginnings, recorded in Scripture must be of tremendous significance to us.

Saint Paul

A Church which claims to "continue" in the Apostles' doctrine and fellowship cannot distance itself from the letters of St. Paul, "the Apostle of the Gentiles" (*Rom.* 11:13; *2 Tim.* 1:11) and the principal writer of the Apostolic Church. His letters were written probably twenty or more years before the oldest Gospel. This means that St. Paul's letters were composed and circulated while many eyewitnesses of our Lord's ministry were still alive; they bring us very close to Christ and the earliest Apostolic Tradition.

St. Paul was a highly educated and well-spoken man, trained in Greek philosophy and steeped in Jewish law, "an Hebrew of the Hebrews" (*Phil.* 3:5), brought up "at the feet of Gamaliel, and taught according to the perfect manner of the law of the fathers" (*Acts* 22:3). But more important than his academic background and credentials is the fact that he was obedient to the commandments of God in Christ. He was faithful to the divine order and eager for the Church to be equally faithful: "Let all things be done decently and in order" (*1 Cor.* 14:40).

"Let your women keep silence"

In this order, St. Paul tells us that Bishops and deacons must be "the husband of one wife" (*1 Tim.* 3:2, 12; *Titus* 1:6).

---

[1]*Book of Common Prayer*, p. 553. The italics are mine.
[2]Irenaeus, *Adversus haereses*, III.4.1.

29

Obviously Apostolic ministers are male: husbands and not wives.

St. Paul also admonishes that women should "keep silence in the churches" (*1 Cor.* 14:34).[1] This Pauline injunction, which many of us believe is a Dominical injunction, is not a prohibition against women singing hymns or joining in common prayers and responses or even reading lessons or prophesying. Dr. Nils Johansson interprets *lalein en te ekklesia* ("to speak in church") as "to give an address at the service" or "to act as teacher at worship."[2] It is a prohibition against women holding the official teaching and sacramental authority of the Church, of presiding over Word and Sacrament, of giving official, authoritative instruction. In *First Timothy*, the Apostle explains: "But I suffer not a woman to teach, to usurp authority over the man, but to be in silence" (2:12). According to the medieval philosopher, Johannes Duns Scotus (c. 1264-1308), St. Paul says "I suffer not [I do not permit] because Christ does not permit."[3]

Could it be that the Pauline injunction about silence is really a Dominical injunction, a saying of Jesus which the Apostle knew? In *First Corinthians*, St. Paul certainly claims that this rule is not of his own devising but among "the commandments of the Lord" (14:37). Origen (*c.* 185-254) spoke of a "command" with respect to this passage.[4] This would strongly suggest that the Apostle is conveying what he knew to be the Lord's will, not simply insisting on the practice of the synagogue or harping on his personal views or idiosyncrasies. Elsewhere in his epistles, there are parallel statements indicating that St. Paul, in his teaching and disciplining, is clearly acting on commandments

---

[1]For a very full discussion of this phrase, see Nils Johansson, *Women and the Church's Ministry*, trans. C. J. de Catanzaro (Ottawa, 1972), pp. 51-89.The Very Revd. Dr. Nils Johansson served as Professor of New Testament at the University of Lund before he was appointed Dean of Linköping Cathedral. Also, one should see Manfred Hauke's scholarly insights: *Women in the Priesthood?*, pp. 363-396.

[2]Nils Johansson, *Op. cit.,* p. 53 & p. 83.

[3]J. Duns Scotus, *Opus Oxoniense*, IV, d. 25, q. 2.

[4]Origen, cited in M. Hauke, *Women . . .*, pp. 389-90. The passage appears in a fragment published in the *Journal of Theological Studies,*10 (1909), 41f.

from Christ *(1 Cor.* 7:10 and *1 Thess.* 4:2,15); also there are clear statements when St. Paul is setting forth his own regulations, and not the Lord's (*1 Cor.* 7:10-12, 25). With good reason, we can take St. Paul at his word and accept that the injunction to silence as indeed "a commandment from the Lord."

If this were so, this would explain why St. Paul, who broke with many Jewish customs, insisted on this particular tradition, not just at Corinth but in all his congregations. It is important to realize that in this passage, St. Paul is not talking about local custom in a particular congregation or group of churches but about the universal practice of the Apostolic Church: "as in *all* churches of the saints" (*1 Cor.* 14:33).

Also it is important to realize that St. Paul, like our Lord, was deeply appreciative of the ministry of women. The Apostle refers to Phoebe as "our sister" (*Rom.* 16:1), calls Priscilla and Aquila "my helpers," and acknowledges that they "laid down their own necks" for him (*Rom.* 16:3-4). In another epistle he writes of "those women which laboured with me" (*Phil.* 4:3). Regardless of what any Women's Lib group may claim, neither our Lord's nor St. Paul's understanding of the role of women in the Church stems from personal bigotry or sexism. Their views are related to divine, and therefore good, order.

Headship Argument

For St. Paul, God's order of creation, as set forth in *Genesis,* clearly establishes the headship of man over woman. The Apostle tells the Corinthians: "But I would have you know, that the head [*kephale*] of every man is Christ; and the head [*kephale*] of the woman is the man: and the head [*kephale*] of Christ is God" (*1 Cor.*11:3). Again, in *Ephesians,* he writes: "For the husband is the head of the wife, even as Christ is the head of the church" (5:23). It is because man is head of the woman, that woman must not "usurp authority over the man" (1 Tim. 2:12). God, in His "eternal and inviolable appointment," says John Calvin (1509-64), "did not create two 'heads' of equal standing."[1]

[1]John Calvin, *Commentary, 1 Tim.* 2:13.

These Pauline passages are not Apostolic prescriptions for male superiority and domination, men "lording" over women, men being domineering or dictatorial, or, God forbid, men oppressing, mistreating or abusing women. St. Paul clearly admonishes: "Husbands, love your wives, even as Christ also loved the Church, and gave himself for it" (*Eph.* 5:25). What amazing, selfless love husbands must strive to imitate!

The Apostle's teaching on headship does provide an Apostolic prescription for how Christian marriages and families, including church families or congregations, are to operate. Once again this is not part of St. Paul's personal eccentricity but constitutes what "is fit in the Lord" (*Col.* 3:18). The man is "head of the woman" and head of the household, *paterfamilias*.[1] This is why traditionally and symbolically he sits at the head of the table and says grace at meals, just as Hebrew fathers for centuries have presided at the Passover Meal, just as Christ presided at the Last Supper, just as He commissioned the Twelve to preside at the Eucharist, and just as the Apostles' successors have presided for 2,000 years. Apostolic Ministers stand at the head of the eucharistic table, with an authority entrusted to them by our Lord, representing the Fatherhood of God and the Headship of Christ.

St. Paul, in his charge to the Ephesian Elders, reminds them that they must function as "overseers" (*Acts* 20:28), a pastoral authority which they have received not from men but from God. Bishop Thomas Brett (1667-1744), in his study of Church Government, quotes this passage from *Acts* as proof of the divine authority for the Apostolic Ministry:

> It is certain Church-Officers derive their Authority from Heaven, and not from the People, because St. Paul expressly declares as much to the Elders of Ephesus, saying "Take heed, therefore unto yourselves, and to all the flock, over the which the Holy Ghost hath made you overseers" (*Acts* 20:28).[2]

---

[1]The fact that in many households fathers may be deceased or absent does not eradicate the biblical understanding of the ideally ordered household.

[2]Thomas Brett, *An Account of Church Government* (London, 1710), I, 8. Dr. Brett was a Non-juror Bishop and distinguished liturgical scholar.

32

St. Paul underscores this shepherding or headship role when he tells the Elders that those who "rule well" should "be counted worthy of double honour" (*1 Tim.* 5:17). He also points out that a Bishop's ability to rule the church is linked to his ability to keep order in his own household (*1 Tim* 3:5 & *Titus* 1:6). Similarly, St. Peter notes that Elders must take "oversight" (*1 Pt.* 5:2).

Given this New Testament background, it is not surprising that our Prayer-book Form of Consecrating Bishops speaks of "government in the Church of Christ," and that the Induction Service speaks of the new incumbent's "Cure of Souls" or "charge," and identifies him as "your Minister who is set over you in the Lord."[1] Neither should we be surprised that the Prayer-book refers to the bishop as "Reverend Father in God"[2] or that George Herbert speaks of the parish priest as "father to his flock."[3] For similar reasons, Vatican documents speak of bishops and priests as standing *in persona Christi capitis* ("in the person of Christ the head").[4]

Women, neither biologically nor spiritually, can really represent God the Father or Christ the Son. They cannot be called "Father." They cannot, according to Pauline teaching, occupy the place of authority and oversight in the Church, the fatherly role required of Apostolic Ministers. They cannot represent and exercise a ministry of headship. Such a ministry, according to the French theologian, Fr. Louis Bouyer, is "a

[1]*Book of Common Prayer,* pp. 662, 669, 671, & 676. The Prayer-book's Ordering of Priests speaks of the laity "who shall be committed to your charge" (pp. 649, 651, & 652) and "over whom they shall be appointed thy ministers" (p. 654).

[2]*Ibid.,* pp. 556, 638, 645, and 660.

[3]George Herbert, *A Priest to the Temple,* Ch. XVI. Herbert writes: "The Country Parson is not only a father to his flock, but also professeth himself thoroughly of the opinion, carrying it about with him as fully, as if he had begot his whole Parish."

[4]Decree *Presbyterorum Ordinis* (7 December, 1965), 2. This term also appears in *The Ordination of Women,* the Official Commentary on *Inter Insigniores* (Catholic Truth Society, 1977), p. 19. *Presbyterorum Ordinis* speaks as well of the priestly ministry as "the office of Christ the Head and the Shepherd" (6).

vocation which, like that of the Head itself, belongs to men only."[1] Long before these words were penned, St. Bonaventure (1221-74) argued that it was precisely because Christ is "Head of the whole Church" that He was incarnate as a male. For Christ to have been incarnate as a female would, according to Bonaventure, have been "a perversion of the order of things [*perversio ordinis*],"[2] that is, an overturning of divine Headship.

The Holy Trinity

In making the biblical argument that man is head of the woman, St. Paul reminds us that "the head of every man is Christ" and "the head of Christ is God." The Apostle roots his discussion of sexual roles in fundamental theology, at the very centre of the Doctrine of the Trinity. During the tenth Lambeth Conference, in 1968, Archbishop Marcus Loane of Sydney, reminded his fellow bishops of this significant fact. He pointed out that "equality and subordination exist in the Trinity side by side": God the Father eternally begets, and Christ is the begotten Son of the Father. "There is," said Dr. Loane, "a distinction in function as there is in human life."[3] Similarly Dr. Graham Leonard, when he was Bishop of London, wrote: "For the Christian, an equality which is based on a diversity is seen, as in the heart of God himself."[4] The principles of equality and subordination, grounded in the Holy Trinity, are not mutually exclusive, irreconcilable ones, but part of the Oneness of God.

The ordination of women, therefore, calls into question the principle of equality and subordination, not only in the created order, but in the divine life of the Blessed Trinity. Such an ordination, according to Archbishop Loane, "would be in conflict with the doctrine of the Godhead." Likewise, Fr.

[1]Louis C. Bouyer, " Christian Priesthood and Women," in *Man, Woman, & Priesthood*, ed. P. Moore, p. 65.

[2]Bonaventure, *Commentarii in quatuor Libros Sententiarum Petri Lombardi*, III, d. 12, a. 3, q. 1.

[3]Marcus L. Loane, cited in J. B. Simpson & E. M. Story, *The Long Shadows of Lambeth X (McGraw-Hill, 1969), p. 191.*

[4]Graham Leonard, *The Bishop of London's Newsletter*, November, 1985, No. 34.

Michael Harper argues that the roles between men and women in creation cannot be interchanged any more than the roles between the Father and the Son can be interchanged in the Trinity. To reverse the God-given roles by ordaining women, he writes, "lifts the false banner of egalitarianism, and waves it in the face of God."[1]

The Pauline comparison of equality and subordination in the sexes to that between God the Father and God the Son underscores the fact that subordination or submission is not about inferiority. St. Paul's statement that "the head of Christ is God" is most definitely not about inferiority or, for that matter, superiority. In the words of the Athanasian Creed, "the Godhead of the Father, and of the Son, and of the Holy Ghost is all one, the glory equal, the majesty co-eternal."[2] As Dr. Roger Beckwith has written, "there is certainly nothing degrading in the internal relationships of the Holy Trinity."[3] Neither is there anything degrading in the headship of man over woman.

Galatians in Context

Advocates of women in the Apostolic Ministry often cite *Galatians* 3:28 as an all-sufficient proof text for their position: "There is neither Jew nor Greek, there is neither bond nor free, there is neither male nor female: for ye are all one in Christ Jesus." If this were a text in support of women's ordination (which is *not* the case!), then it would be difficult to harmonize this passage with many other sayings of St. Paul already cited. It is true that in this verse St. Paul celebrates our spiritual equality in Christ, or more correctly, our "oneness" in Christ.[4] But in so doing he is not engaging in reductionism; he is not denying the reality of ethnicity (Jew and Greek) nor the reality of the civil order (slave and free); and he is most definitely not denying the reality of the created order (male and female), nor the specific order of Christ's Church. Fr. George Rutler, in

[1]Michael Harper, *Equal and Different*, p. 158.
[2]*Book of Common Prayer*, p. 695
[3]Roger Beckwith, *"The Bearing of Holy Scripture,"* p. 50.
[4]The Greek word *eis* correctly translates "one," not "equal."

35

a delightful passage, says that St. Paul

> is not clapping his hands to announce a genetic revolution. "Neither male nor female" is no more a statement of natural biology or psychology than "neither bond nor free" is sociology or "neither Jew nor Greek" is anthropology. In the same sense, when we sing "In Christ there is no east or west," we do not mean to find pagodas in Sioux City.[1]

The Apostle, therefore, is not saying that Baptism obliterates the distinction between the sexes, overturns the order of the Church, and erases her diversity of functions. He is not making a case for women to be bishops any more than he is making a case for men to be child-bearers or paving the way for male nuns.[2] Rather he is speaking about the baptismal covenant and the essential oneness we have in the Body of Christ.

The two preceding verses of *Galatians* provide the context: "For we are all the children of God by faith in Christ Jesus. For as many as have been baptized into Christ Jesus have put on Christ" (3:26-27). Women have the same baptismal dignity as men and are not second-class citizens in our Lord's spiritual Kingdom. Women have full and complete membership in the Church; they share with men fully in the priesthood of all believers, which is "a royal priesthood" (*1 Pt.* 2.9). Fr. Michael Harper explains that both men and women are

> made in the image of God and share equally in the glories of being created by God, redeemed by Christ, and filled by the Holy Spirit. They both share freely in the riches of God's grace, and will share equally in the glories of eternal life.[3]

Ordination bestows no greater dignity or privilege than this.

[1]George W. Rutler, *Priest and Priestess* (Trinity Press, 1973), p. 21. Fr. Rutler, who was an Anglican priest and rector, is now a Roman Catholic priest.

[2]Apparently a new religious order of transsexual nuns does function in Los Angeles, California, with Sister "Boom-Boom" as superior! This is a startling reminder of what can happen when there is confusion about God's order in creation and in His Church. Sometimes extreme examples help us to see the basic underlying problem.

[3]Michael Harper, *Equal and Different,* p. 204.

In fact, the priestly vocation is about servanthood, not about clericalism, and definitely not about status, power, or control. In his great study of the priesthood, Dr. R. C. Moberly (1845-1903) comments on the nobility of the laity in the Old Testament: "But to Israel of old, to be 'the People' of God was the height of positive privilege." *Laos*, says Moberly, "is the word of most positive spiritual privilege, the glory of covenanted access to and intimacy with God."[1] Ordination can convey no greater dignity, no better status, no higher vocation in God's Kingdom than this.

However, none of this is to say that women and men are the same or that both can be priests. The dignity of women is certainly not enhanced by stressing only their humanity and blurring all sexual distinctions. The doctrine of the priesthood of all believers is not enhanced by ordaining every baptized person and allowing everyone to perform the same functions within the Body of Christ. As Bishop Michael Marshall has written, "The phrase 'the priesthood of all believers' is not the same as the priesthood of every believer."[2]

The Body of Christ

Within the Body of Christ, God has called and appointed male Apostles to minister. "And he gave some apostles; and some prophets; and some evangelists; and some, pastors and teachers: for the perfecting of the saints, for the work of the ministry, for the edifying of the body of Christ" (*Eph.* 4:11-12). For the well-ordering and functioning of the body, a certain divine order has been imposed and specific tasks within the body appointed.

The analogy of the human organism and its parts is thoroughly worked out by St. Paul in the twelfth chapter of *First Corinthians*, where he is talking about "diversities of gifts" and "differences of administrations" and "diversities of operations"

[1]R. C. Moberly, *Ministerial Priesthood, 2nd ed.* (John Murray, 1913), p. 98.

[2]Michael Marshall, *Glory Under Your Feet: The Challenge of Catholic Renewal Today* (Darton, Longman & Todd, 1978), p. 93.

(vv. 4-6). Diversity of calling and function in the Church is compared with diversity in the human body, in which different parts and organs have different purposes. All cannot be feet, hands, eyes, or ears. Neither are the parts interchangeable; a hand cannot be a foot, nor an eye an ear. All are necessary parts of the whole; all are required for the well-functioning of the entire organism (12:14-26).

The particularities or differences of the individual members, in either the human body or the spiritual body of Christ, are significant. The Apostle tells the Corinthians: "Now ye are the body of Christ, and members *in particular*" (27). That means that all are *not* Apostles or prophets or teachers (29). Christian equality, oneness in Christ, is not about equality of function, everyone doing the same thing. All must humbly accept their God-appointed places and not covet another's role or imagined status. And not for a moment can it be forgotten that Christ is the Lord of the Church, her Master, her chief cornerstone, "the head of the body" (*Col.* 1:18). The Church must always be subordinate, humbly obedient to her Lord.

Humble Service
Humility, which is at the heart of Christian ministry, begins with our Lord Himself, who, says St. Paul,
> made himself of no reputation, and took upon him the form of a servant and was made in the likeness of men: And being found in fashion as a man, he humbled himself, and became obedient unto death, even the death of the cross (*Phil.* 2:6-7).

This humility, says the Apostle, we must imitate: "Let this mind be in you, which was also in Christ Jesus" (v. 5).

The Twelve Apostles -- even Judas, who failed miserably -- were called to humble service. On Maundy Thursday, our Lord gave them an extraordinary and radical example of service; He knelt as a servant and washed their feet (*Jn.* 13:4-9). When James and John sought choice seats in Christ's kingdom, He lectured them and the other Apostles about servanthood and discipleship: "Whosoever will be great among you, let him be your minister; and whosoever will be chief among you, let him be your servant"

(*Mt.* 20:26-27; see also *Mk.* 10:42-45 and *Lk.* 22:24-27). The Apostles' role of headship and superintendence in the community of faith was to be understood as humble service, not as prideful domination.

Bishop Jeremy Taylor says that Christ set the Apostles "over the household, not to strike the servants, but 'to give them their meat in due season.'" He quotes St. Optatus (*fl.* 370), Bishop of Milevis, in North Africa: *non dominium sed ministerium* ("nothing of dominion but of ministry," that is, of service). In an eloquent passage, Dr. Taylor continues:

> And indeed we need challenge no more: it is honour enough to serve such a Prince, to wait at such a table, to be stewards of such a family, to minister such food. This service is perfect freedom; and that is more than can be said of the greatest temporal dominion in the world.[1]

The Apostolic Ministry, though most honourable and esteemed, is never about exalted status or human rights; it is always about humble service in the Body of Christ and perfect freedom in Him.

The Bride of Christ

Headship and the Body are not the only biblical images of Christ's divinely-ordered relationship to His Church; another image, of great significance, is that of marriage. Just as in the Old Testament God is described as the Bridegroom of Israel (*Ps.* 45 & *Isa.* 54:6), so Christ identifies Himself as the Bridegroom (*Mt.* 9:15; *Mk.* 2:19; see also *Jn.* 3:29). In the parable of the ten virgins, our Lord describes His appearance as that of a bridegroom at a wedding feast (*Mt.* 25:1-13). John the Baptist identifies himself as "the friend of the bridegroom," the best man (*Jn.* 3:29).

St. Paul speaks of espousing his Corinthian Church "to one husband, that I may present you as a chaste virgin to Christ" (*2 Cor.* 11:2). In teaching the Ephesians about the sacred relationship between husbands and wives (5:22-32), St. Paul

---

[1]Jeremy Taylor, *Ductor Dubitantium* (1660), III, 4.1.6. The passage from St. Optatus is from his *Contra Parmenianum Donatistam,* V.

likens a husband's sacrificial love to that of Christ for His Bride, thereby speaking "concerning Christ and the church" and disclosing   "a great mystery" (32). As divine Bridegroom, Christ "loved the Church, and gave himself for her" (25). On the cross, the Bridegroom shows His unparalleled love for His bride; He husbands His church;   He gives himself for her.   In *Revelation*, St. John describes the eschatological church, that is, the heavenly church in Jerusalem, as "the bride" and "the Lamb's wife,"   "coming   down from God, out of   heaven" (19: 7 & 21:2,9). This nuptial imagery is God-given, part of God's revelation. As Fr. John Saward explains: "God has set his seal on some images, and not on others, for his revelation, and we must gratefully and humbly accept *his* choice."[1]

The use of spousal or bridal imagery for the Church is common throughout the Christian Tradition. Bishop John Jewel (1522-71), the great apologist or defender of the claims of the Church of England, writes:

> And that this Church is the kingdom, the body, and the spouse
> of Christ;   and that Christ alone is the prince of this kingdom;
> that Christ alone is the head of this body;   and that Christ alone
> is the bridegroom of this spouse.[2]

We are conscious of such imagery every time we sing the well-known hymn, "The Church's one foundation":

> From heaven he came and sought her
>   To be his holy Bride,
> With his own blood he bought her,
>   And for her life he died.[3]

Our Lord's bride, the Church, whom we properly refer to with feminine pronouns, is also our fruitful, life-producing mother. St. Cyprian (d. 258), Bishop of Carthage, exclaims that "You cannot have God for your Father if you have not the Church for your Mother."[4] St. Ambrose refers to the Church as

---

[1]John Saward, *Christ and his Bride*, p. 9
[2]John Jewel, *Apologia Ecclesiae Anglicanae*, II.
[3]S. J. Stone (1839-1900), "The Church's one Foundation," St. 1, lines 5-8.
[4]Cyprian, *De ecclesiae catholicae unitate*, 6.

"Eve, the mother of all living." In this passage, St. Ambrose links the creation of Eve from the side of Adam to the creation of the Church, from the side of Christ, from "the rib of the second Adam," from the water and blood which flowed from the spear-wound. In each case, "Eve, the mother of all living," is created. "Let God come then," says St. Ambrose, "let Him build woman, the first as the help-mate of Adam, the last as that of Christ."[1]

A Bridegroom Ministry

This marriage of Christ and His beloved, what the Prayer-book Marriage Service calls "the mystical union that is betwixt Christ and his Church,"[2] has serious implications about the ordaining of women. When a priest stands in the place of Christ at the altar -- the most important thing that a priest does -- he is symbolically representing or imaging the Bridegroom, who on the cross sacrificed Himself for His bride. Pope John Paul II, in one of his Apostolic Letters, calls the Eucharist "the Sacrament of the Bridegroom and the Bride."[3] Fr. John Saward writes: "The Body given in the Eucharist is the Body given on the cross, the Body of the Bridegroom pouring out his love and life for the Bride. That supreme mystery can only be imaged by a man."[4] As I have explained elsewhere, Christ's role as bridegroom is mightily symbolized in the Easter Vigil Rite when the priest plunges the candle into the font, the life-bearing womb of the Church. God the Father, through the Son, descends upon the water of Baptism and makes His Bride fruitful, life-producing.[5]

For a woman to occupy the position of groom suggests something very unnatural indeed, and turns God's plan upside

---

[1] Ambrose, *Expositio Evangelii secundum Lucam*, II, 86ff. John Saward makes much of this passage in his tract, pp. 7-8.
[2] *Book of Common Prayer*, p. 564. The Prayer-book Ordinal speaks of the Church as Christ's "spouse and body" (p. 649).
[3] John Paul II, *Mulieris Dignitatem* (St. Paul Books, 1988), p. 89.
[4] John Saward, *Christ and his Bride*, p. 12.
[5] G. R. Bridge, "Lecture on the Solemn Rites of the *Triduum Sacrum*," King's College Chapel, 26th March, 1997.

down. This shocking reversal of created and natural relationships underscores the gravity of trifling with things that are God's order, things that are deeply mystical, and beyond our understanding. We dare not underestimate the damage caused by tampering with what we do not, and can not, fully comprehend.

In an essay opposing women priests, that consummate Anglican writer, C. S. Lewis (1898-1963), makes this point exceptionally well: "We have no authority to take the living and semitive figures which God has painted on the canvas of our nature and shift them about as if they were mere geometrical figures."[1] Lewis argues that human sexuality has psychological and spiritual dimensions which are beyond reason and which quickly take us out of our depth. In the Church, he writes,

> we are dealing with male and female not merely as facts of nature but as the live and awful shadows of realities utterly beyond our control and largely beyond our direct knowledge. Or rather, we are not dealing with them but (as we shall soon learn if we meddle) they are dealing with us.[2]

The Authority of Scripture

Thus far in this book I have been staying very close to arguments from Scripture, and demonstrating why I think that Scripture is neither silent nor inconclusive on the matter of women in the Apostolic Ministry. There are certainly other convincing arguments for me, and I shall examine these briefly in the remaining pages. But Scripture must come first, and classical Anglicanism has always said so. Scripture, declares Article VI, "containeth all things necessary to salvation"; and what can not be proved by Scripture "is not to be required of any man."[3] Article XX concedes that the Church has authority

---

[1] C. S. Lewis, "Priestesses in the Church?" (1948), in *God in the Dock,* ed. W. Hooper. (Grand Rapids, 1970), p. 238. This collection of essays was printed in England as *Undeceptions.*

[2] *Ibid.,* p. 239.

[3] *Book of Common Prayer,* p. 700. Roger Beckwith considers Article VI one of the three Articles "on which all the others really turn." See "The Prayer Book and Evangelical Doctrine," in *The Prayer Book,* ed. G. R. Bridge (St. Peter's Publications, 1985), p. 75.

to decree rites and settle controversies of Faith, but emphasizes that "it is not lawful for the Church to ordain any thing that is contrary to God's word written."[1]

According to the Prayer-book Ordinal, deacons, priests, and bishops all affirm that the Holy Scriptures contain sufficiently all doctrine required of necessity for eternal salvation through faith in Jesus Christ."[2] Following the laying on of hands, the newly ordained are presented with a Bible;[3] they are entrusted with its care and also reminded, in a very tangible way, of its primacy and its authority in the ministry they are called to exercise.

This biblical emphasis is not, of course, a kind of mindless fundamentalism but is simply a recognition of the authority of Holy Scripture, which is at the heart of Anglicanism. All Anglicans -- women and men, bishops and laity -- are called to live under the authority and judgement of Holy Scripture. The importance of the Bible should be obvious to any who have experienced worship according to *the Book of Common Prayer*. Its liturgical formularies are centred in the Word of God, and generous portions of every Prayer-book service consist of scriptural lections. Dr. Oliver O'Donovan points out that the reading of Scripture, not its exposition, is at the heart of Anglican worship: "the books of Scripture are not authoritative because the church views them in a certain way; the church views them in a certain way because they are authoritative."[4]

Has the Anglican Church forgotten that the Scriptures are indeed authoritative? It is my firm conviction that parts of the Anglican Church have proceeded with the ordination of women because they have biblical amnesia. They have forgotten, ignored, or repudiated the teachings of Holy Scripture; they

[1]*Ibid.*, p. 706. Article XXXIV also counsels "that nothing be ordained against God's Word" (p. 711).

[2]*Ibid.*, pp. 641, 651, and 663.

[3]Deacons are presented with the New Testament; bishops and priests receive both Testaments.

[4]Oliver O'Donovan, *On the Thirty Nine Articles* (Paternoster, 1986), p. 50.

have abandoned the Apostles. They have, knowingly or not, turned their backs on God's order of creation and redemption, and have done what our Lord accused the Pharisees and Scribes of doing: "Full well ye reject the commandment of God, that ye may keep your own tradition" (*Mk.* 7.9). St. Paul warned the Colossians of taking this same man-made road: "Beware lest any man spoil you through philosophy and vain deceit, *after the tradition of men,* after the rudiments of the world, and not after Christ" (*Col.* 2:8).

I would close this chapter with chilling and prophetic words, written in 1948 by Dr. Kenneth E. Kirk (1886-1954), a distinguished and scholarly Bishop of Oxford (1937-54):

> Those who plead recklessly for the ordination of women should be urged to turn back to their Bibles, and ask themselves how they are able to reconcile their cherished but ill-regulated enthusiasm with the clear teaching which they find there.[1]

How indeed?

[1] Kenneth E. Kirk, *Beauty and Bands,* ed. E. W. Kemp (Hodder and Stoughton, 1955), p. 188.

2. Tradition

What do we mean by Tradition?

Tradition with a capital *T* is not about preserving local customs or idiosyncrasies, not about antiquarian pursuits and hobbies; this is tradition with a small *t*. It is not about beating the parish bounds in Rogationtide, or having pancakes on Shrove Tuesday, as venerable and delectable as these customs may be to some of us. It is not simply a matter of canonical discipline, about whether clergy are allowed to marry or if they must retire at sixty-five. It is not even about women wearing veils or hats![1] Rather, Tradition (Gk. *paradosis;* Lat. *traditio* = "give over" or "hand down"*)* is a vital, living, transmission from one generation to another of those things held most sacred and essential. Tradition, therefore, is "the continuous stream of explanation and elucidation of the primitive faith . . . the accumulated wisdom of the past."[2] It involves not merely decades but generations and centuries.

Early in the Church's life, St. Irenaeus (*c.* 130-200), Bishop of Lyons, writes that if there is a theological dispute among us, "should we not have recourse to the most ancient churches with which the Apostles held constant intercourse, and learn from them what is certain and clear on the issue?" In the event that no Apostolic writings are available, he asks: "Should we not in that

---

[1]St. Paul's rule about veils (*1 Cor.* 11:2-16) is a good example of a transitory practice, a relatively unimportant, small-*t* tradition, which is local and temporary, and for which there is no universal Tradition. Dr. Hauke says that head-covering is "obviously not an essentially necessary component of the *depositum fidei*" (p. 348).

[2]*Oxford Dictionary of the Christian Church,* ed. F. C. Cross & E. A. Livingstone, 2nd ed. (Oxford University Press, 1983), pp. 1388-89.

case, follow the course of the Tradition which they handed down to those to whom they committed the churches?"[1] This is surely the Apostolic Tradition in word and in deed.

A century before St. Irenaeus, St. Paul describes the Apostolic Tradition by telling the Corinthians: "For I delivered unto you first of all, that which I also received" (*1 Cor.* 15:3).[2] Likewise, he admonishes: "keep that which is committed to thy trust" (*1 Tim.* 6.20). St. Vincent of Lerins (d. before 450), in a gloss on this Pauline passage, explains that this keeping is "not that which thou hast thyself devised"; it a not a matter "of wit, but of learning; not of private adoption, but of public tradition."[3]

The Solemn Declaration
A modern example of this serious notion of Tradition in action is found in the Canadian Church's *Solemn Declaration*, 1893. The bishops, together with the clergy and lay delegates, at the First General Synod, 1893, declare their desire to receive

> the One Faith revealed in Holy Writ and defined in the Creeds . . . the same Canonical Scriptures of the Old and New Testaments . . . the same Divinely ordained Sacraments through the ministry of the same Apostolic Orders . . . the Doctrine, Sacraments, and Discipline of Christ . . . in the Book of Common Prayer . . . and in the Thirty-nine Articles of Religion . . . and to transmit the same unimpaired to our posterity.[4]

This fervent desire to receive and to transmit "unimpaired" the Apostolic deposit is what Tradition is all about. We are not the creators of Apostolic Tradition but the inheritors, caretakers, and transmitters of it.

An essential part of the Apostolic deposit is the Apostolic Ministry, what the *Solemn Declaration* calls "Apostolic Orders."

[1]Irenaeus, *Adversus haereses*, III.4.1.
[2]St. Paul makes a similar statement just before his account of the Last Supper and his recording of the Words of Institution: "For I have received of the Lord that which also I delivered unto you" (*1 Cor.* 11:23).
[3]Vincent of Lerins, *Commonitorium,* xxii.
[4]*Book of Common Prayer,* p. vii.

The lineage of these Orders is most venerable. As Bishop Charles Gore, C.R. (1853-1952), writes:

It is, in fact, impossible to exaggerate the intimacy with which the episcopal succession is bound up with the fixed canon of Scripture and the permanent and stable creed to constitute what may rightly be called 'historical Christianity.'[1]

The Tradition of Male Clergy

The Tradition of the Church has constantly affirmed the biblical teaching that the Apostolic Ministry is restricted to males. This means that the Church for over nineteen and a half centuries, including her most turbulent and revolutionary periods, has persistently and faithfully ordained only males, and thus has remained in step with the teaching and practice of the Apostles themselves.

The earliest written evidence we have of this Tradition outside of Scripture is the already-quoted *First Epistle* of St. Clement of Rome, written in 96 A.D., about a generation after the deaths of Saints Peter and Paul. St. Clement speaks of a male succession in the Apostolic College, noting that the Apostles themselves appointed *men* to succeed to their ministry and thereby established permanence or continuity: "when these men die, other approved men shall succeed to their ministry."[2] Likewise, St. Irenaeus (*c.* 130-200) claims that he can "enumerate those who were by the Apostles instituted bishops in the churches, and the succession of these *men* to our times."[3] Tertullian (*c.* 160-225) notes: "It is not permitted for a woman to speak in church, nor yet to teach, nor to anoint, nor to make the offering, nor to claim for herself any office performed by man or any priestly ministry."[4]

Later Patristic authorities agree with the earliest Tradition. The *Apostolic Church Order* (*c.* 300), states: "When the Master

[1]Charles Gore, *The Ministry of the Christian Church*, 2nd ed. (Rivingtons, 1889), p. 216. "Development of language and form," writes Gore, does not "involve any change of principle or belief."
[2]Clement, *I Corinthians* 44.4.
[3]Irenaeus, Adversus haereses, III.3.4.
[4]Tertullian, *De virginibus velandis*, 9.1.

47

prayed over the bread and the cup and blessed them saying, 'This is my Body and Blood," he did not allow women to stand with us."[1] St. Epiphanius (315-403), Bishop of Salamis, surveys the Orders of both the Old and New Covenants and concludes: "God never appointed to this ministry a single woman upon earth."[2] St. John Chrysostom (c. 347-407), Bishop of Constantinople, in his book on priesthood, says that "divine law excluded women from this ministry."[3] The *Apostolic Constitutions* (late 4th C.) clearly denounce women presbyters: "For this is one of the ignorant practices of the Gentile atheism, to ordain women priests to the female deities, not one of the Constitution of Christ."[4] St. Augustine (354-430), Bishop of Hippo, writes that the priest "is a *man* who administers to the people the Mystery and the word of God."[5] The Council of Laodicea (365) states that "Presbytides, as they are called, or female presidents, are not to be appointed in the church"; and further directs: "Women may *not* go to the altar."[6] Pope Gelasius, in 494, condemns any priestly acts by women, acts "performed by the sex that has no right to do so."[7] The Council of Trullo (692), says: "Women are not permitted to speak at the time of the Divine Liturgy."[8]

The medieval scholastic theologians were consistent in their teaching that women could not be the recipients of Holy Orders. St. Thomas Aquinas (c. 1225-74), "the Angelic Doctor," argues that the male sex is required for both the "lawfulness" and the "validity" of Holy Orders; a woman "cannot receive the Sacrament of Order."[9] Aquinas clearly accepted the Pauline

[1]*Apostolic Church Order*, 24. Here the Apostles are speaking and recalling Christ's own teaching.

[2]Epiphanius, *Panarion*, 79.7.4.

[3]John Chrysostom, *De sacerdotio*, 3.9. See also 2.2: "Let all womankind give way before the magnitude of the task -- and indeed most men."

[4]*Apostolic Constitutions*, III.9.

[5]Augustine, *Epistola*, 21.

[6]Council of Laodicea, Canons XL and XLIV, which were ratified by the Council of Chalcedon (451).

[7]Gelasius, *Epistola*, IX. 26.

[8]Council of Trullo (The "Quimsext" Council), Canon LXX.

[9]Thomas Aquinas, *Summa Theologia*, III, q. 39, a. 1.

notion of headship, which forbade women from either teaching or sacramental authority. Earlier he says that women, if they "have the grace of wisdom or of knowledge, can administer it by teaching privately but *not publicly*."[1] St. Bonaventure (1221-74), "the Seraphic Doctor," argues that since the priest signifies Christ as Mediator or Head, "the capacity for receiving ordination is therefore appropriate only for men."[2] Johannes Duns Scotus (*c.* 1264-1308), "the Subtle Doctor," states that the prohibition against women priests comes directly from our Lord: "Christ alone first prescribed this, he who instituted the sacrament."[3]

The Continental Reformers, who disposed of many things (far too many!), nevertheless, continued the Tradition of a male ministry. John Calvin (1509-64), in the best Pauline tradition, argues that women cannot exercise the preaching and teaching offices, which have to do with "oversight" and which are "inconsistent with being in subjection." He writes: "For how unsuitable it would be for a woman, who is in subjection to one of the members, to have pre-eminence and authority over the whole body."[4] Elsewhere, he says that women must not baptize:

> The practice before Augustine was born is first of all inferred from Tertullian, who held that a woman was not allowed to speak in the church, and also not to teach, to baptize, or to offer. This was that she might not claim for herself the function of any man, much less that of a priest.[5]

Calvin also notes that the Council of Carthage (under Gratus, *c.* 348) decrees that women "should not presume to baptize at all."[6]

[1]*Ibid.*, II. II, q. 177, a. 2. In very similar fashion, John Calvin explains: "Paul is not taking from women their duty to instruct their family, but is only excluding them from the office of teaching (*a munere docendi*), which God has committed exclusively to men" (*Commentary, 1 Timothy 2:11*).

[2]Bonaventure, *Commentarii in quatuor Libros Sententiarum Petri Lombardi,* IV, d. 25, a. 2, q. 1.

[3]Johannes Duns Scotus, *Opus Oxoniense,* IV, d. 25, q. 2.

[4]John Calvin, *Commentary, 1 Corinthians* 14:34. In another place, Calvin calls the government of women "an unnatural monstrosity." He explains: "Thus for a woman to usurp the right to teach would be a sort of mingling of earth and heaven" (*Commentary, 1 Timothy 2:12*).

[5]John Calvin, *Institutes,* IV.15.21.

[6]*Ibid.,* IV.15.20.

The Anglican Tradition

Although Richard Hooker (*c.* 1554-1600) took a less strident position on whether laywomen could baptize, he nonetheless firmly upheld the Pauline injunctions concerning women's ministerial role in the Church. He writes: "To make women teachers in the house of God were a gross absurdity, since the Apostle has said, "I permit not a woman to teach; and again, "Let your women in churches be silent."[1] Bishop Jeremy Taylor cites many ancient authorities upholding the male Apostolic Ministry, but ultimately he too refers women desirous of Orders to St. Paul. Dr. Taylor writes: "I remit them to the precept of the Apostle: 'But I suffer not a woman to teach, but to be in silence.'"[2] This biblical viewpoint of Hooker and Taylor, in step with the Tradition of the whole Church, East and West, certainly remained the Anglican position until the closing decades of our present century. Even Archbishop William Temple (1881-1944) admitted that to extend the priesthood to women would be "most certainly contrary to all the laws and precedents of the church."[3]

One of the principal Christian apologists of our century, C. S. Lewis (1898-1963), said that the ordination of women would be "a revolutionary step," making us "cut ourselves off from the Christian past," and "would be an almost wanton degree of

---

[1]Richard Hooker, *Of the Laws of Ecclesiastical Polity*, V.62.2.

[2]Jeremy Taylor, *Of the Office Ministerial*, 3.7. Bishop Taylor says that whatever deaconesses did in the early Church, "they could not speak in public, unless they did prevaricate the Apostolical rule given to the Corinthian and Ephesian Churches" (*Ibid.*).

[3]William Temple, cited in Harold Riley, "Women as Priests?," in *Sexuality - Theology - Priesthood*, ed. H. K. Lutge (Fellowship of Concerned Churchman, n.d.), p. 7. On a personal level, Dr. Temple apparently favoured the idea of women priests; however, he knew that it would drastically push back the cause of Christian unity; and, unlike many bishops today, he refused to make this issue more important than the unity of Christ's Church. In a letter of March, 1916, he wrote to a priest's wife about his true priorities in this regard: "But still more do I want to see real advance towards the re-union of Christendom and the general emancipation of women." Cited in F. A. Iremonger, *William Temple, Archbishop of Canterbury: His Life and Letters* (Oxford University Press, 1948), p. 452.

imprudence."[1]   In a preparatory paper for the Tenth Lambeth Conference (1968), Dr. Alan Richardson (1905-75), then Dean of York, noted that the ordination of women "would not be reverting to an ancient practice (as, for example, restoring the Cup to the laity), but would be making an innovation for which there was no ancient or ecumenical precedent."[2]   Dr. Eric Mascall (1905-1993), an eminent theologian, has written about the ordination of women:

> Of all the innovations that have been introduced or proposed in the long history of the Christian Church it would be difficult to find one more extreme than this, or more clearly in conflict with the traditional Anglican attitude on matters of faith and practice.[3]

Dr. Eric Kemp, the present Bishop of Chichester and an authority on canon law, has said that he cannot recall any other occasion in history when the English Synod

> has been invited to reject a universal tradition of the Catholic Church.   Neither the rejection of papal authority, nor the abolition of the rule of clerical celibacy in the sixteenth century, is comparable.   Neither of these was the rejection of a universally held tradition.[4]

Heresies

Until modern times, the only exception to a male ordained ministry was among certain heretical sects.   In the second century, Gnostics (from Gk. *gnosis* = "knowledge"*)*, claimed to have a private *gnosis* or secret knowledge, that is a private tradition apart from Holy Scripture. These Gnostic heretics or Marcionites (followers of Marcion), also later known as Marcosians (followers of Marcus), rejected out of hand the biblical account of creation. They ascribed creation to a lesser god (Demiurge), who was quite separate from the supreme spiritual God, the Divine Being.   They did not know the supreme

[1]C. S. Lewis, "Priestesses in the Church?," p. 235.

[2]Alan Richardson, cited in J. B. Simpson & E. M. Story, *The Long Shadows of Lambeth X*, p. 190.

[3]E. L. Mascall, "Some Basic Considerations," in *Man, Woman, & Priesthood*, ed. P. Moore, p. 10.

[4]E. W. Kemp, addressing General Synod, 3 July, 1975.

God as a personal Deity but as an "ineffable," unknowable Father or Mother.[1]

Gnostics believed that Christ was a divine messenger who brought redeeming *gnosis* with Him. He did not really assume a human body, let alone a male body, nor suffer nor die; he temporarily inhabited another body or made phantasmal, ghost-like appearances. This aspect of Gnosticism, mentioned on p. 18, is called Docetism (from the Greek word for "seem"). Christ seemed or appeared to be a man, but He really wasn't; he seemed to suffer but really didn't. Such Docetic teaching was a denial of the Doctrines of the Incarnation and Atonement, including a repudiation of Christ's birth as a male and His death on the cross as a male.

Gnostics believed that in the order of redemption all natural, physical distinctions, such as sexuality, were abolished; the divine seed or spark in man was liberated, rescued from the flesh and from the evil environment of the material world. Sexual differences, therefore, were something to be despised and overcome. As Fr. Rutler has humorously pointed out, post-lapsarian Adam and Eve, shocked by their nakedness and sexual differences, "proceeded to dress themselves in the academic robes of the world's first Docetists: Figleaves."[2]

The Gnostics' disdain for sexual distinctions is abundantly evident in their literature, which often speaks of the interchangeableness of the sexes. For example, the Gnostic *Gospel of Thomas* (*c.* 200), rejected by the early Fathers, attributes this heretical saying to Jesus:

[1]The influential Gnostic Valentinus (2nd C.), founder of the Valentinians, taught that God was a Dyad consisting in one part of the ineffable Father and in another as the Silence of the Womb, "the Mother of All" (Irenaeus, *Adversus haereses*, I,11.1.). Followers of Valentius prayed to Silence for her protection as Mother. Marcus, a disciple of Valentius, taught that Silence was the Source of Grace and that the wine of the Eucharist symbolized her blood (1.14.1). It should be noted that Gnostic systems can be remarkably different and complex.

[2]George W. Rutler, *Priest and Priestess*, p. 15.

When you make the two one, and when you make the inside like the outside and the outside like the inside, and the above like the below, and when you make the male and the female one and the same, so that the male be not male nor the female female . . . then you will enter the kingdom.[1]

Such anti-sexual teaching is equally anti-masculine and anti-feminine. Often anti-feminine views are more pronounced. In the same Gnostic Gospel, for instance, Peter asks that Mary be excluded from their circle because of gender, and Jesus responds by saying that he will make her into a male: "For I tell you truly, every female who makes herself male will enter the kingdom of heaven."[2]

Given this Gnostic teaching, or lack of biblical understanding of creation and redemption -- that creation is not of God, that God is impersonal and cannot be known as Father, that feminine symbolism can be indiscriminately used for God, that the Incarnation and Atoning Death of Christ were nothing more than visions, that Christ was not really born as a male, that all natural distinctions like sexuality are unimportant in redemption, that the sexes are interchangeable, that Scripture may be discarded or corrected, etc. -- it is easy to see how Gnosticism could entertain the notion of women priests. All these things are related, both in the second and in the twentieth centuries.

Another early heresy, Montanism (followers of Montanus), a zealous apocalyptic movement, looking for the immediate fulfilment of the last days, also allowed women clergy. Closely associated with Montanus were many prophets and prophetesses, including a prominent female leader, Priscilla, who claimed to have seen a vision of Christ as a woman. Likewise the Collyridians, a fourth-century idolatrous cult to the Blessed Virgin Mary, allowed priestesses. They sacrificed cakes (colluris) to Mary and then consumed them.

Each of these heretical sects abandoned the clear witness of

[1]The Gospel of Thomas, 22.
[2]Ibid., 114.2

Scripture and the following of the Apostles, in far more than the ordination of women. Indeed, the ordination of women was only symptomatic of a larger problem, as it is today. Each of these groups was castigated by the early Fathers, who were eager to uphold the biblical and Apostolic view.[1] Typical is the remark by St. Epiphanius (c. 315-403), Bishop of Salamis, concerning the Montanists: "they ignore the word of the Apostle."[2]

In time these sects and their women clergy all died out; and until our present situation have remained but aberrations, odd footnotes, in the broad sweep of Catholic history. The whole Church did not accept the eccentricities of these heresies or cults and adhered to the biblical and orthodox pattern of male presbyters. For many of us that Tradition must still stand; we are not persuaded by the arguments of Gnosticism in our own day.

The Vincentian Canon

A classical, threefold test of Tradition is the rule or canon of St. Vincent of Lerins (d. before 450), which states: *Quod ubique, quod semper, quod ab omnibus creditum est* ("What has been believed everywhere, always, and by all").[3]

If we apply this threefold test of universality (ubiquity), antiquity, and consent to the ordination of women, it is obvious that this innovation fails miserably as a Tradition of the Church. In fact, it would be difficult to find a better test case than this. Dr. Eric Mascall has written that "if there is anything to which the Vincentian Canon does apply absolutely, it is surely the restriction of priesthood to the male sex."[4] Likewise, Bishop

---

[1] A brief survey of the patristic response to these heresies will be found in Manfred Hauke, *Women in the Priesthood?*, pp. 404-423. Hauke also mentions that women clergy were found among two medieval sects: the Cathari (from the Greek word for "pure") and the Waldenses, who likewise claimed to hold a pure and uncorrupted version of Christianity (pp. 106 & 467).

[2] Epiphanius, *Adversus haereses*, 49.3.

[3] Vincent of Lerins, *Commonitorium*, II.3.

[4] E. L. Mascall, "Some Basic Considerations," in *Man, Woman, & Priesthood*, ed. P. Moore, p. 11.

Kallistos Ware has written: "If ever there was a practice that contravened the Vincentian Canon, it is certainly the ordination of women to the priesthood."[1]

Consensus Fidelium

When the Vincentian Canon speaks of consent, it is talking about the *consensus fidelium*, the consent of the faithful. This is not present-day consent, like the Canadian electorate showing consensus in their voting for a particular political party and a few years later arriving at a new consensus and voting for another party. *Consensus fidelium* is about the collective mind of the Church Catholic or Universal, how the Church has consistently lived under the teaching and authority of Scripture, not for the short run but for the long haul. It is not about what the Church happens to believe at the present moment, or at any isolated moment in history, but what has been believed universally, "everywhere, always, and by all." As the Archbishops' Report on Doctrine states:

> The weight of the *consensus fidelium* does not depend on mere numbers, or on the extension of a belief at any one time, but on continuance through the ages and the extent to which the consensus is genuinely free.[2]

This kind of consensus or Tradition is about being in step with our ancestors in the Faith, not simply "touching base" with them, but receiving from them the Faith "which was once delivered" (Jude 3) and passing it on "unimpaired"; it is about avoiding isolation, not being cut off from our past. G. K. Chesterton (1874-1936) explains Tradition as "an extension of the franchise":

> Tradition means giving votes to the most obscure of all classes, our ancestors. It is the democracy of the dead. Tradition refuses to submit to the small and arrogant oligarchy of those who merely happen to be walking about.[3]

[1]Kallistos Ware, "Man, Woman, and the priesthood of Christ," *Ibid.*, p. 70.

[2]*Doctrine in the Church of England* - The Report of the Commission on Christian Doctrine appointed by the Archbishops of Canterbury and York (SPCK, 1938), p. 35. The 1948 Lambeth Conference, in its Report on "the Anglican Communion," quotes this passage (SPCK, 1948), p. 85.

[3]G. K. Chesterton, *Orthodoxy* (John Lane, 1912), p. 83.

In humility, today's Church must be willing to give the vote to those who have gone before: to the Apostles, to our forebears in the Faith, to great scholars and theologians who have articulated the theological Tradition. Their perspective, their consensus, must inform our own position. And if anyone is worried about acting with the majority, rest assured that all the faithful now at rest most definitely constitute the real majority!

Anglicans as Catholics

This belonging to the Communion of Saints, the Church living and departed, saves us from a narrow and sectarian view of the Church, from seeing her only in terms of our own specific time and place, our own passions and pet projects. This in large measure is what it means to belong to the Catholic Church, the Universal Church, the Church in continuity with the Apostles.

Anglicans, in their ecclesiology (study and understanding of the Church) have always maintained that they are a loyal part of the larger Church, the Church Catholic. Hence, Bishop Thomas Ken (1637-1711) could eloquently testify in his will: "I die in the Holy Catholic and Apostolic Faith, professed by the whole Church before the disunion of East and West. . ."[1]   In more recent times, Archbishop Geoffrey F. Fisher (1887-1972), who crowned our present Queen, boldly asserted: "We have no doctrine of our own -- we only possess the Catholic doctrine of the Catholic Church enshrined in the Catholic creeds. . ."[2]   Ken and Fisher belong to a long and distinguished line of Anglican churchmen, who have understood what it means to be Catholic, to be in step with the Catholic Church through the ages, to be part of a great Tradition, to give the vote to those who have gone before, long before the English Reformation of the Sixteenth

[1]Thomas Ken, in his will (1711).   He continues the statement: "more particularly I die in the Communion of the Church of England, as it stands distinguished from all Papal and Puritan Innovations, and as it adheres to the doctrine of the Cross." Cited in F. A. Clarke, *Thomas Ken* (Methuen, 1896), p. 223.

[2]Geoffrey F. Fisher, in a speech delivered in the Central Hall, Westminster, 30th January, 1951.   Cited in Anselm Hughes, *The Rivers of the Flood* (Faith Press, 1961),   p. 50.

Century. Incidentally, we number Archbishops of Canterbury from St. Augustine (597), not Thomas Cranmer (1532). Dr. Carey is the 103rd, not the 35th, Archbishop of Canterbury!

This profession of Catholicism has certain implications about the ordained ministry and Sacraments, that is, about those things which most distinguish the Anglican Communion from a number of Protestant Churches. Archbishop Cyril F. Garbett (1875-1955) wrote: "A Church to be Catholic must hold the Catholic Faith, treasure the Catholic Scriptures, administer the Catholic Sacraments, and retain the Catholic Ministry."[1] Anglicans have Catholic -- not Anglican or Protestant! -- Sacraments and Orders.

Being Catholic, then, is not simply a matter of playing "Mr. Dress-up" or "Ms. Dress-up" and doing as one pleases, blissfully ignorant, or blissfully defiant, of Catholic Tradition. Liturgical clothes and gestures, and all the incense in the world, do not make one a Catholic! Catholics are those who are in step with the whole Catholic Church, who cherish the Catholic Scriptures, Creeds, Sacraments, and Orders. Sadly there are those among us who call themselves "Catholic" and who embrace novelties like the ordination of women, same-sex marriages, inclusive language for the Deity, and so forth. They are like Lewis Carroll's Humpty Dumpty, who explains to Alice his subjective use of language: "'When *I* use a word,' Humpty Dumpty said in a rather scornful tone, 'it means just what I choose it to mean -- neither more nor less.'"[2] In light of 2,000 years of Catholic Tradition, such self-proclaiming, self-defining Catholicism is powerfully unconvincing; it sorely lacks both objectivity and credibility.

The Catholic Priesthood
In the Sixteenth Century, Anglicans did not invent or create a new Protestant ministry but continued the threefold Apostolic Orders of Catholicism. Dr. Sparrow Simpson (1859-1952)

---

[1]Cyril Garbett, *The Claims of the Church of England*, (Hodder & Stoughton, 1947), p. 17.
[2]Lewis Carroll, *Through the Looking-Glass* (1871), Ch. 5.

57

speaks of the Anglican Church's "deliberate retention" of Catholic Order.[1]   Richard Hooker summarizes the matter well:

> I may securely therefore conclude that there are at this day in the Church of England no other than the same degrees of ecclesiastical order, namely Bishops, Presbyters, and Deacons, which had their beginning from Christ and His blessed Apostles themselves.[2]

The Preface to the Prayer-book Ordinal states that the ancient Apostolic Orders of Bishops, Priests, and Deacons are to "be continued, and reverently used and esteemed."[3] The Archbishops of Canterbury and York, in their Reply to Pope Leo XIII on Anglican Orders (*Apostolicae Cura*, 1896), cited the Preface to the Ordinal as proof of

> the intention of our Anglican Fathers to keep and continue these offices which came down from the earliest times, and "reverently to use and esteem them," in the sense, of course, in which they were received from the Apostles and had been up to that time in use.[4]

If, as the Preface to the Ordinal claims, the Apostolic Ministry is not exclusively ours but that of the whole Church Catholic, then that ministry should be easily recognized by those who have gone before. Bishop Kenneth Kirk makes this point especially well:

> So it is every bit as important for us that we should have a ministry which would be recognized as such by the Church of all the ages as that we should have one which would be recognized by Christian denominations of today. The unity of the Body of Christ, though organic, must transcend all limitations of time and space.[5]

[1]W. J. Sparrow Simpson, *The Ministry and the Eucharist* (SPCK, 1942), pp. 85 and 94.

[2]Richard Hooker, *Of the Laws of Ecclesiastical Polity*, V.78.12.

[3]*Book of Common Prayer*, p. 637.

[4]*Responsio*: "The Reply of the English Archbishops to the Bull *Apostolicae Curae* of Pope Leo XIII" (1897), XVII. The Latin *Responsio* was composed by Bishop John Wordsworth (1843-1911), of Salisbury.

[5]K. E. Kirk, *"How Necessary Are These Orders?,"* in *Beauty and Bands*, p. 249. This essay is about the relationship between the Anglican Church and Churches without episcopal Orders.

And so those who would admit women to the Apostolic Ministry must ask if this innovation would be recognized by those who have preceded us in the Catholic Faith: by Christ and the Apostles? by the Early Fathers? by the Medieval Schoolmen and the Reformers? by classical Anglican theologians? by Cranmer, Jewel, Hooker, Laud, Taylor, Keble and Pusey? even by great Anglican thinkers of our own Century -- by Lewis, Kirk, and Mascall? Should we not listen to what they have to say about women in the Apostolic Ministry? Should we not give votes to them?

The Development of Tradition?

Tradition is not something relegated to the dusty shelves of rare book rooms but is a living thing and therefore does not remain static. Tradition grows and develops, with new insights and understandings, but it does not develop randomly, or indiscriminately; it cannot whimsically overthrow Scripture. Jesus told the Apostles that the Spirit would lead them into all truth and would call to mind what Jesus Himself had taught them. The Holy Spirit does not contradict Himself; He does not talk out of both sides of His mouth.

Within classical Anglicanism, the development or progression of doctrine has definite parameters. The Council of Trent (1545-1563) went far beyond those parameters in asserting that Scripture and Tradition have equal authority. Likewise, John Henry Newman, exceeded the parameters in his *Essay on the Development of Christian Doctrine* (1845), written a few months before he left the Anglican Church and became a Roman Catholic. In this book, Newman attempted to explain why he could accept as legitimate theological development certain Roman Catholic teachings which were not found in Scripture or the Tradition of the early Church. In classical Anglicanism, as set forth in the Articles and the early apologists like Jewel, Hooker, and Laud, Tradition cannot supersede Holy Scripture, which is the primary authority of the Church. The Lambeth Quadrilateral of 1888 reaffirms this Anglican position that the Holy Scriptures contain "all things necessary to salvation" and are "the rule and ultimate standard of faith."[1]

The Doctrine of the Holy Trinity is an example of genuine development within the biblical Tradition of the Church. Although the actual word *Trinity* is never used in Scripture, the concept of the Trinity is certainly to be found therein. Hence, the elaboration of this doctrine by the early Church Fathers is not the overthrow of scriptural teaching, not a radical departure from the Bible, but rather a development which is wholly consistent with Scripture and the teaching of the Apostles.

The Tradition of Holy Orders, as mentioned earlier, underwent a development in the first 150 years of the Church's life. Much of this development is seen within the pages of the New Testament, where more than one name is used for the same order of ministry (Apostle, Bishop, Elder, and Presbyter). What is clear is that by the end of the first century, the Apostolic Ministry was in place. Indeed the threefold ministry is older than some canonical books of the Bible. Early in the second century, shortly after the Apostolic Age, the universal Apostolate developed into local bishoprics. The letters of St. Ignatius show that this pattern was well established by the time of his death (*c.* 107). Historians differ on exactly how this entire process occurred, but by 150 it was the norm throughout the Christian Church, and remained the unquestioned norm until the Reformation fifteen hundred years later.

Not only did this development occur very close to the time of the Apostles, but it was wholly consistent with Scripture, a natural and faithful development, not a departure from it. Archbishop Michael Ramsey (1904-1988) writes: "Developments thus took place, but they were all tested." Scripture, Dr. Ramsey insists, "has a special authority to control and to check

[1]The Quadrilateral, which was Resolution 11 of the 1888 Lambeth Conference, sought, through its four short articles, to establish the essential ground, including "the Historic Episcopate," for reunion with other churches. The Lambeth Quadrilateral was a slightly revised version of the Chicago Quadrilateral, passed by the Episcopal Church, U.S.A., in 1886.

the whole field of development in life and doctrine," and he notes that the second-century theologians who dwell most on church order, St. Ignatius and St. Irenaeus, "are precisely those whose whole theology is most controlled and pervaded by Scripture."[1]

The ordination of women, on the other hand, is not a development which is consistent with either Scripture nor the Tradition of the Church. It is a novelty, an innovation, practiced heretofore only by heretical sects and by Protestant Churches not claiming to hold the three-fold Apostolic Ministry nor any theology of Catholic priesthood. More than a development, it must be seen as a very serious break with Tradition. In an open letter to Archbishop Robert Runcie in December, 1988, Pope John Paul II wrote that the Roman Catholic, Orthodox, and Oriental Orthodox Churches were all "firmly opposed to this development, viewing it as a break with Tradition of a kind we have no competence to authorize."[2] Archbishop Donald Robinson, the former Anglican Archbishop of Sydney, Australia, has written that the male Apostolic order of the New Testament, received and practiced by the Churches of the East and West, "is not a tradition which is capable of development. It can be discarded, but not developed."[3]

Why?

Given the consistent Tradition of the Church that the Apostolic Ministry is male, why should Anglicans suddenly be intent on breaking that Tradition, on departing from the practice of the centuries, from going out, very far out, on a limb?

Reverence for Tradition has made many Anglicans, even those favouring the ordination of women, uneasy. A good example is

[1]Arthur Michael Ramsey, *The Gospel and the Catholic Church* (Longmans,1936), p. 64.

[2]His Holiness Pope John Paul II to the Most Revd. Robert Runcie, 8th December, 1988, printed with the Eames Report (Church House, 1989), p. 38.

[3]Donald Robinson, "Scripture, Apostolic Tradition, and the Ordination of Women," in *The Evangelical Catholic*, XIII, No. 4 (January, 1990), p. 1.

the Report of the 1968 Lambeth Conference on the ordination of women. Although the Report finds "no conclusive theological reasons" against women priests, it makes this strong cautionary note:

> The appeal to Scripture and tradition deserves to be taken with the utmost seriousness. To disregard what we have received from the Apostles, and the inheritance of Catholic Christendom, would be most inappropriate for a Church for which the authority of Scripture and tradition stands high.[1]

Perhaps the answer to why parts of the Anglican Church have abandoned Scripture and Tradition and proceeded with the ordination of women lies in social and political movements of our day, in what some perceive as justice or equal rights issues. I shall address some of these matters briefly in a later section of this book. At this juncture, it must simply be underscored that the ordination of women is a radical departure from the Tradition of the Church. Hence, C. S. Lewis, a moderate and cautious churchman, called it "revolutionary," and Dr. Mascall, a systematic theologian, called it "extreme."

Women Saints & Leaders

In spite of this long and consistent Tradition that the Apostolic Ministry is male, the Church through the ages has been greatly blessed by a number of outstanding women, who have made a very substantial contribution to the life of the corporate Body. God has raised up many women saints, and called them to a variety of vocations. Some like St. Perpetua (d. 203) and St. Agnes were early martyrs for the Faith. St. Helena (c. 255-330) went to the Holy Land and discovered the true cross. Many, like St. Clare (1194-1253) and St. Bridget of Sweden (c. 1303-73), have witnessed to God through the religious or conventual life. Some have exerted enormous influence beyond the cloister walls; one recalls St. Hilda (614-80), Abbess of Whitby, who was a prime player at the Synod of Whitby (664), or St. Hildegard

[1]*The Lambeth Conference 1978: Resolutions and Reports* (SPCK, 1968), p. 106. The Chairman of Subcommittee 21 on Women and the Priesthood was Archbishop W. W. Davis of Nova Scotia.

(1098-1179), who was an advisor to emperors, kings, and prelates. Some, like St. Margaret of Scotland *c.* 1045-93*)*, were queens. Some, like St. Monica (*c.* 331-87*)*, were exemplary mothers. Some, like St. Julian of Norwich (*c.* 1342-1413), St. Catherine of Sienna (1347-80), and St. Theresa of Avila (1515-82), have been great mystics, the latter two being declared Doctors of the Church. In our own century, God has raised up Mother Teresa of Calcutta (1910-97). He has also raised up great Anglican scholars and writers like Evelyn Underhill (1875-1941) and Dorothy L. Sayers (1893-1957).

There is no question but that women can, and have, served the Church with great distinction, erudition, and holiness of life. In spite of the remarkable gifts that these women and others have offered to the Church, there is no record that any one of them was ever in Apostolic Orders or desirous of the same. Mother Teresa, who was an outspoken opponent of women priests, believed most emphatically that "women have other things to do." Church history and the theological Tradition would certainly support her thesis.

3. Sacramental Theology

Gifts of God

Sacraments, including Holy Orders, are God's own gifts to the Church Catholic. They are divinely appointed or instituted, as is the Church herself. They depend not on us or any synodical authority but on the will of God, who empowers and engraces them. Hence, Richard Hooker says that Holy Orders are "not from men," and Jeremy Taylor says that they are "not of human provision."[1] Fr. T. T. Carter (1808-1901), a venerable, sub-Tractarian divine, writes of Holy Orders: "A Priest is one who, not by any merit, or virtue, or power of his own, but by the will of God, has been made a necessary link in the chainwork of the Divine purposes."[2] Likewise, our most famous Anglican liturgiologist, Dom Gregory Dix (1901-52), teaches that "the sacramental power and authority which come by ordination are from above, not from below, from God, not from a 'recognition by the Church.'"[3]

The Givenness of Sacraments

Sacraments are part of the givenness of the Catholic Faith. They are among the happiest of gifts, and they ought to be received most humbly and gratefully from Christ and His Apostles. They certainly are not ordinances received from the contemporary Church; they are not mere indulgences granted by our subjective, power-hungry, and revisionist synods. Sacraments do not simply make us feel good; they ought not to make us wallow in the subjective and ephemeral; they are not

[1]See p. 10 for references.

[2]T. T. Carter, *The Doctrine of the Priesthood in the Church of England*, 2nd ed. (Joseph Masters, 1863), p. 99.

[3]Gregory Dix, *Holy Order* (Church Literature Association, 1976), p. 25.

65

part of what T. S. Eliot calls "the general mess of imprecision of feeling, / Undisciplined squads of emotion."[1] Sacraments are too objective and real, too trustworthy, for such nonsense.

A revealed, incarnational, and historical religion like Christianity must put great stock in that which is objectively given, that which lies beyond, and is independent of, our subjective apprehensions. The great spiritual guide, Baron Friedrich von Hügel (1852-1925), says that he came more fully to this understanding, indeed reached it "with entire clarity," between the first (1908) and second editions (1923) of his impressive, two-volume work on St. Catherine of Genoa (1447-1510). As important as we human subjects are, says von Hügel, the reality of the Object of religion ("itself the Subject of all subjects") is what essentially matters:

> . . . its Givenness is the central characteristic of all religion worthy of the name. The Otherness, the Prevenience of God, the One-sided Relation between God and Man, these constitute the deepest measure and touchstone of all religion.[2]

And so it is with the givenness and objectivity of the Sacraments, whose Reality is beyond anything we can fathom or fashion.

Sacraments and the Incarnation

The Incarnation, the Eternal Word made flesh, is the supreme Sacrament, from which all others flow. Each Sacrament is like the Incarnation, or is an "extension" of the Incarnation, in that it is "an outward and visible sign of an inward and spiritual grace."[3] Like the Incarnation, the Sacraments have material manifestations, outward particularities, which are not arbitrary, optional, or interchangeable. In each and every detail, the Sacraments are God's; He is their Giver and only source.

St. Clement of Rome, for example, writes to the Corinthian Church:

[1]T. S. Eliot, *East Coker*, V, lines 181-82.
[2]Friedrich von Hügel, *The Mystical Element of Religion as Studied in Saint Catherine of Genoa and Her Friends*, 2nd ed. (J. M. Dent & Sons, 1923), Vol. I, p. xvi.
[3]The Catechism, *Book of Common Prayer*, p. 550.

Where and by whom He desires these things to be done, He Himself has fixed by His own supreme will, in order that all things being piously done according to His good pleasure, may be acceptable unto Him.[1]

Please note that St. Clement's proper concern is not that sacramental administrations will be acceptable unto us but rather unto Christ, their Founder and Institutor, the Supreme Sacrament Himself, our true and only High Priest. Our opinions pale in comparison with His perfect, unqualified knowing.

Because the Sacraments are God's, not ours, we cannot meddle with them. We cannot play about with them as though they were mere business items on the agenda of some synod or parish council. Dr. Robert Crouse, in an excellent ordination homily, teaches that Holy Orders

are established in the Word of God; and therefore they are not just matters of institutional convenience, to be adopted, or altered, or discarded, according to our whim, or according to the dictates of worldly prudence, or according to the temper of the times. They are the gifts of Christ, the Risen and Ascended Lord, "for the perfecting of the saints, for the work of the ministry, for the edifying of the Body of Christ" (*Eph.* 4:12).[2]

Article XXXIV does allow that national churches "hath authority to ordain, change and abolish ceremonies or rites of the Church ordained only by man's authority."[3] Sacraments, however, are much more than ceremonies or rites, much more than liturgical texts or orders of service. The latter can certainly be revised from time to time, even if not to our liking. Sacraments, on the other hand, are divine, not man-made, ordinances. Therefore, we have no authority to change them.

The Catholicity of the Sacraments

Because Anglicanism embraces the Tradition of the whole

[1]Clement, *1 Corinthians,* 40.3.

[2]R. D. Crouse, Homily preached at the Ordination of the Revd. John Paul Westin to the priesthood, 24th June, 1987, St. Peter's Church, West LaHave, Nova Scotia. Reprinted in *the Anglican Free Press* (Christmas, 1987), p. 9.

[3]*Book of Common Prayer*, p. 712.

Church, it upholds the sacramental life and practice of the whole Church, Catholic and Apostolic. Anglicans have no Sacraments of their own but only those of the undivided Church: the two Gospel or Dominical Sacraments of Baptism and the Eucharist, and the five "lesser" Sacraments, including the Sacrament of Orders.

Thus, Anglicans have always been able to claim that their priests are priests of the Universal Church and that every Eucharist celebrated by them is a Eucharist of the whole Church. According to the Prayer-book Ordinal, a priest is not ordained in the Anglican Church but "in the Church of God."[1] "Since the Church is universal," writes Dr. C. B. Moss (1888-1964), "she requires a ministry which is universally recognized."[2] The 1938 Report on Doctrine states that the priest acts "not only on behalf of the individuals who may at the moment be worshipping but of the whole community within which they so worship."[3] Dr. E. J. Bicknell (1882-1934) stresses the larger context, the whole communion of Saints, both the Church Militant and those whose work is done:

> Every true Eucharist is a Eucharist not just of the few Christians gathered within the walls of a building, but of the whole Church, living and departed. Hence the minister must possess authority to act not simply as minister of one part of the Church but as the minister of the whole.[4]

The Anglican-Roman Catholic agreed statement on the ministry states that "every individual act of ordination is therefore an expression of the continuing Apostolicity and Catholicity of the whole Church."[5]

[1]*The Book of Common Prayer*, p. 655. Bishop Robert Martineau comments on the universality of the priest's office: "His priesthood is of the Church of God, not of any one part of it only." *The Office and Work of a Priest*, rev. ed. (Mowbrays, 1981), p. 31.

[2]C. B. Moss, *The Christian Faith: An Introduction to Dogmatic Theology* (SPCK, 1943), p. 382.

[3]*Doctrine in the Church of England* (SPCK, 1938), p. 156.

[4]E. J. Bicknell, *A Theological Introduction to the Thirty-Nine Articles*, 3rd ed. (London, 1959), pp. 330-31.

[5]"Ministry and Ordination" (1973), 2.14, in *The Final Report* (Forward Movement, 1982), p. 36.

Since a number of Anglican Provinces have broken with the Catholic and Apostolic Tradition by ordaining women, can they still claim that their Orders are those of the Universal Church? Can a Eucharist celebrated by a woman really be a Eucharist "of the whole Church, living and departed"? How could we possibly assume this universality when female celebrations cannot be fully recognized in our own parishes and dioceses, let alone in the wider Anglican Communion? How can we pretend that "sacraments" celebrated by women priests are those of the Universal Church?

Again and again in this matter, we seem, like Esau, to have sold our birthright for a "pottage of lentils" (*Gen.* 25:34). We have lost the larger picture and have settled for something considerably smaller and less Catholic, something which has no precedence in Scripture or Tradition, including the Church's canon law.

Immutable Canon Law

In his noteworthy book on canon law, Bishop Robert Mortimer (1902-77) distinguishes between mutable or changeable canon law and that which is immutable or unchangeable. Dr. Mortimer notes that "apart from fundamental moral precepts the most important part of the immutable canon law concerns the validity of the Sacraments."[1]

Traditional Sacramental theology, as set forth in immutable canon law, teaches that there are five conditions for a valid Sacrament, all of which must be correct: matter, form (words), subject (recipient), minister, and intention (doing what the Church does). The particularities of Sacraments are important, just as the particularities of creation and redemption are important, just as the particularities of the Incarnation, including our Lord's sexuality, are important. Dr. C. B. Moss likens a valid Sacrament to a legal cheque, which must be written on the bank's specified form, dated correctly, signed by the right person,

[1] R. C. Mortimer, *Western Canon Law* (Adam and Black, 1953), p. 76.

et cetera, in order to be recognized and honoured by the bank.[1]

Neither Anglicanism nor any other Catholic Church has the authority to write bogus cheques, to change or alter the incarnational details or particularities of the Sacraments, which are immutable, unchangeable, unwavering. No matter what any Lambeth Conference or General Synod may attempt to do, the Anglican Communion as a whole -- let alone any of its national churches -- does not have the competence or authority to make revisions to the Sacraments, which God has specifically appointed and graciously given to His Church.

Hence, some well-meaning but grossly mistaken synod cannot increase or reduce the number of Sacraments. Neither could it change the matter of the Sacraments. It could not substitute other fluids, like cholrox or green paint, for the water of Baptism, nor beer and pretzels or coke and cookies for the bread and wine of the Eucharist. It could not decide that if grapes are the essence of the Eucharist, we could use grape juice instead of grape wine. In fact, Anglicans have been quite fussy about insisting upon "pure grape wine,"[2] and not even sherry, which is a fortified wine and not "pure."

Neither does Anglicanism have authority to alter the proper subject or recipient of a Sacrament. It could not decide that mammals, rather than human beings, could receive Baptism and then start baptizing pet cats, dogs, baboons, and orangutans. Neither can it decide to marry two people of the same sex although that practice has its persistent, modern-day advocates. Likewise, it has no competence to ordain women to Apostolic Orders.

Bishop Mortimer says that ordination requirements concerning age and education may be altered by the Church, but that the sexual requirement of a man and not a woman "admits of no alteration or exception, because that is part of the determination

---

[1]C. B. Moss, *The Christian Faith*, p. 335.
[2]*Book of Common Prayer*, p. 74.

by the Church of what is divinely required for the validity of the Sacrament of Orders."[1] The Canon Law of the Roman Catholic Church states: "Only a baptized man can validly receive sacred ordination."[2] The Canon Law of the Eastern Orthodox Church states: "A woman does not become a priestess (*presbutéra*)."[3] Until recently, the Canon Law of the Anglican Church required male ordinands, and thus was in step with the great ancient churches of both East and West.

Invalid Orders?

It is a grave matter that parts of the Anglican Communion have abandoned Catholic sacramental Tradition, overstepped canonical bounds of authority, and permitted its synods to alter God-given Sacraments. Even more serious is what actually happens or does not happen when such changes are implemented. What becomes of the Sacraments? Are they invalidated?

If one or more of the five requirements for a valid Sacrament is changed, accidentally or intentionally, there can be no guarantee, no assurance, that the altered Sacrament is valid. In other words, one can go through all the sacramental-like actions so that ordinances appear to be Sacraments, but there is no guarantee. Hence, we cannot be sure that women upon whom bishops lay hands in ordination rites are in fact ordained. Their status may not be changed. St. Thomas Aquinas is adamant on this point:

> Wherefore even though a woman were made the object of all that is done in conferring Orders, she would not receive Orders, for since a sacrament is a sign [*signum*], not only the thing [*res*], but the signification of the thing [*signum rei*], is required in all sacramental actions. . . .[4]

Many standard theological textbooks, like those by Dr. Francis

[1] R. C. Mortimer, *Western Canon Law*, pp. 76-77.
[2] *Codex Iuris Canonici*, 1024.
[3] *Nomocanon* of Photius, 1:37.
[4] Thomas Aquinas, *Summa Theologia*, III (Supplement), q. 39, 1. Aquinas compares the requirement of a male in the Sacrament of Orders to the necessity of a sick person in the Sacrament of Unction, who is required "in order to signify the need of healing."

J. Hall (1857-1932) and Dr. C. B. Moss (1888-1964), which have shaped and informed several generations of Anglican priests, consistently teach this. Dr. Hall says: "Neither a woman nor one unbaptized is capable of receiving the character and grace of Order."[1] Dr. Moss states: "The 'subject' of ordination is a male baptized person. . .Women cannot be admitted to Holy Orders."[2]

In addressing the Bishops at the 1978 Lambeth Conference, Canon John Macquarrie, who is no enemy of women's ordination, pointed out to their Lordships that many in the church "conscientiously believe that a woman cannot validly consecrate the Eucharist." And then he makes this parenthetical, but incredibly significant, remark: "And who can prove beyond doubt that such persons are mistaken?"[3]

How does this affect other Sacraments?

The spiritual implications of this are, of course, staggering. If a woman is not the right subject for the Sacrament of Orders, then neither can she be a valid, effective minister for the "sacraments" she attempts to administer. One cannot dispose of sacramental grace without the authority to do so. And how can we be certain that God has reversed His own decisions and policies and granted priestly authority to women? How can one demonstrate in any conclusive way that this innovation is God's will and constitutes the mind of Christ?

If a woman purports to be an ordained priest, and she is not, then the sacramental ministrations she performs are not reliable or guaranteed. Of course, a woman can go through all the right motions -- she can put on vestments, say and chant the liturgy, and make liturgical gestures, and do all these things most competently and gracefully. Competence, or the lack thereof, is

[1]Francis J. Hall, *Theological Outlines,* 3rd ed. (SPCK, 1933), p. 275
[2]C. B. Moss, *The Christian Faith,* p. 387.
[3]John Macquarrie, 1978 Lambeth Conference (Hearing B, 31st July, 1978); LC.78, UKC. No. 105 (*not* in the abridged version of his speech in the Appendix of the 1978 Lambeth Report). In his *Principles of Christian Theology* (Charles Scribner's, 1966), Macquarrie admits his openness to the ordination of women (pp. 386-87).

not the issue. A woman celebrant can even use a traditional liturgy, one that is most pleasing to traditionalists![1]

Notwithstanding all this, we must still ask: Can we know beyond a reasonable doubt that God approves and sanctions the admission of women to His Sacrament of Orders? Do we truly know that God conveys "inward and spiritual grace" through women priests and bishops? Can this radical, man-made revision to God's Sacrament of Orders be trusted? Bishop Jeremy Taylor warns us of the great seriousness of not having divine authorization for the ministry:

> The grace and powers that enable men to minister in the mysteries of the Gospel is so wholly from God, that whosoever assumes it without God's warrant, and besides His way, ministers with a vain, sacrilegious and "ineffective hand," save only that he disturbs the appointed order, and does himself a mischief.[2]

Dr. Taylor insists that the ministry be exercised with "God's warrant," that is, in "His way," not our way. This great Anglican bishop goes on to say that without God's complete endorsement and unqualified commissioning, the ministry is but an empty sign: "Without His appointment, a man must not, cannot any more do, than a messenger can carry pardon to a condemned person which his prince never sent."[3]

The sort of questions, therefore, which every devout communicant must ask are of this most practical yet most spiritual nature: Is spiritual grace actually and objectively conveyed by a woman's sacramental ministrations? Is the absolution she gives

---

[1]St. Firmilian, Bishop of Caesarea (d. 268), talks of a prophetess who "often dared to celebrate the Eucharist, using the correct Liturgy, and in this way deceived many." According to St. Firmilian, a genuine exorcist demonstrated that the woman had really been inspired by an evil spirit (Cyprian, *Letters,* 75.10-11). Bishop R. C. Mortimer relates this story in *The Celebrant and Ministers of the Eucharist* (Mowbray, 1957), pp. 10-11. Dr. Mortimer's book is a classic study of who may celebrate the Eucharist: "a *man* ordained through the laying on of hands of the Episcopate" (p. 3).

[2]Jeremy Taylor, *Of the Office Ministerial,* 6.7 (6.6 in the 1850 edition).
[3]*Ibid.,* 7.2.

genuine? Is it a pardon sent from the Prince Himself? Is the Eucharist she celebrates unquestionably valid? Is the blessing she pronounces over a bride and groom efficacious? Do the candidates confirmed by a woman bishop actually, unconditionally, receive the Apostolic laying on of hands? Do ordinands, even male subjects, receive valid, unambiguous orders from a female bishop? Can there be any doubt about these matters? Can there be any question of defect in these ministrations? Must not Sacraments be totally reliable?

Sure Witnesses?

This element of uncertainty and risk flies in the face of our sacramental theology. Sacraments are, according to Article XXV, "certain sure witnesses, and effectual signs of grace."[1] This belief in the absolute certainty of Sacraments causes Bishop Kenneth Kirk to declare "a first principle" of sacramental theology: ". . . Where the integrity of the sacraments is in question, the Church must always take the safer course, and act on certainties and not on probabilities." Dr. Kirk continues: "It is certain that a duly ordained priest can celebrate the Eucharist validly; it is at best doubtful whether a woman, even if 'ordained,' may do so."[2]

The Eames Commission[3] talks of the need of bishops and dioceses favouring the ordination of women "to understand the problem of the *uncertainty* about a Eucharist presided over by a woman and about ordinations by a woman bishop."[4] The uncertainty is this: nothing in all of Scripture nor Tradition can assure us that "sacraments" conducted by a woman priest or bishop can be "certain sure witnesses and effectual signs."

A Church which holds Sacraments in high esteem cannot take

[1] *Book of Common Prayer*, p. 707.
[2] K. E. Kirk, *Beauty and Bands*, p. 188.
[3] The Archbishop of Canterbury's Commission on Communion and Women in the Episcopate, chaired by the Most Revd. Robert Eames, Primate of All Ireland.
[4] Eames Commission, *Report* (1989), ¶42, p. 20. The italics are mine.

chances with them, cannot live with a sacramental "may-be," "could-be," or "want-to-be." A Church which believes that there is an objective reality to Sacraments cannot reduce them to experimental or provisional ordinances, cannot turn them into a game of Russian roulette.   A Church which takes seriously the cure of souls cannot be sacramentally or pastorally irresponsible, cannot allow her people to receive doubtful Sacraments, cannot risk any spiritual harm.   Souls are far more important than political agendas!

Spiritual danger?

Bishop William Wantland, an authority on canon law, confesses his agnosticism about women priests but his complete and abiding confidence in real Sacraments: "I do not know if a woman can be a priest but I do know that only a priest (or bishop) may offer the Eucharist." He concludes: "It would therefore be a great spiritual danger to allow a celebrant of doubtful validity to function. . . ."[1] Can we flirt with spiritual danger? Can we have anything less than complete confidence about the Sacraments we receive?

Surely the dying penitent deserves to receive the ministrations of a priest in sufficient, well-grounded, and undisputed Orders; that expiring person deserves to receive a valid absolution and valid Holy Communion. But this does not apply only to *in extremis*, near-death cases. On a day to day basis, faithful communicants need to know that they are receiving valid Sacraments, not ministrations which just make them "feel" good but which really make them good, not empty signs, but authentic,

[1]William C. Wantland, quoted from a letter, with the author's permission. In a recent book, Bishop Wantland makes a similar statement: "We Anglicans believe that the Eucharist, like Baptism, is a Sacrament 'generally necessary for salvation' . . . We also believe that only a Priest (or Bishop as High Priest) may offer the Eucharistic sacrifice . . . If (for the sake of argument) a woman cannot, in God's will, be a Priest, then she cannot validly offer the Eucharistic sacrifice, nor am I then fed on the Body and Blood of Christ if I partake of her offering. My soul, no longer sacramentally nourished, is in mortal danger." *The Catholic Faith, the Episcopal Church and the Ordination of Women* (Diocese of Eau Claire, 1997), pp. 20-21.

Spirit-filled Sacraments, which objectively engrace and nourish them, which feed them not merely for the moment but unto eternal life. Listen to the certainty with which our Lord speaks of the Eucharist: "Except ye eat the flesh of the Son of man, and drink his blood, ye have no life in you. Whoso eateth my flesh, and drinketh my blood, hath eternal life: and I will raise him up at the last day" (*Jn.* 6:53-54).

We must be deeply concerned not only for the souls of the laity who receive questionable "sacraments" but for the bishops who tamper and experiment unnecessarily, who desperately try to convey Apostolic order to women subjects, and, of course, for the women clergy themselves. In Jeremy Taylor's words, they all do themselves "a mischief." Dr. Eric Segelberg, in his preface to Dr. Nils Johansson's book, speaks of the cruelty the Church inflicts on women clergy, who can never exercise their ministry fully confident of their orders. He writes:

> Most women who are ordained have read enough theology to realize that their ordination raises problems, and some are very much aware of this. How disastrous it is for the spiritual life of such a person to perform sacred functions day after day in a state of uncertainty of her vocation![1]

We must never forget that Sacraments closely impinge upon the spiritual life of the whole, corporate Church. Modifications to the Sacraments, therefore, have spiritual consequences for all of us.

In the Person of God and of His Son

Before leaving this discussion of Sacraments, something must be said about the Church's traditional understanding of the priest as a sacramental representative of God the Father and Christ the Son. St. Ignatius (*c.* 35-107), Bishop of Antioch, very early in the Church's life, said that "the bishop has the role of the Father."[2] In many places, it is common to call Apostolic

[1] Eric Segelberg, Preface to Nils Johansson, *Women and the Church's Ministry*, p. 10 .

[2] Ignatius, *To the Trallians*, 3.1.

76

Ministers, both bishops and priests, "Father." This is not done because the priesthood is a closed, patriarchal, and hierarchical system, but because part of the vocation of the Church's ordained priests is to represent God the Father and the principles of His Fatherhood. The priest ministers not simply *in persona Dei* ("in the person of God") but more specifically *in persona Patris* ("in the person of the Father") and *in persona Filii* ("in the person of the Son").

In our Prayer Book tradition, we are much aware of the priest as a divine, fatherly representative when he alone stands to pronounce absolution: "Amighty God, the Father of our Lord Jesus Christ. . ." or "Almighty God, our heavenly Father. . ." or "May the Almighty and merciful Lord. . ."[1] The Blessings at the end of the Eucharist and the Confirmation Service are pronounced in the name "of God Almighty, the Father, the Son, and the Holy Ghost."[2] The two priestly blessings in the marriage service are also good explicit examples of this: "God the Father. . ." and "Almighty God, the Father of our Lord Jesus Christ. . . ,"[3] as is the Aaronic Blessing in the Burial Office: "The Lord bless you, and keep you. . . ."[4]

As celebrant of the Eucharist, the priest obviously takes the part of Christ, *persona Christi*, in a sacred drama.[5] St. Cyprian notes that "the priest truly acts in the place of Christ."[6] St. John Chrysostom says that the priest's "part is but to open his mouth," to perform "a symbol."[7] Elsewhere, this great Bishop of Constantinople writes: "The priest stands before us doing what

[1] *Book of Common Prayer*, pp. 5, 20, 77, & 726.

[2] *Ibid.*, p. 86 & p. 561.

[3] *Ibid.*, pp. 567 & 571

[4] *Ibid.*, p. 601. The second funeral blessing is less fatherly in its imagery but has the wonderful reference to "that great Shepherd of the sheep."

[5] This acting in the place of Christ is dramatically evident in the celebrant's taking the part of Christ in the solemn reading of the Passion Gospels throughout Holy Week.

[6] Cyprian, *Epistulae*, 63. 14.

[7] John Chrysostom, *Homilies on 2 Timothy*, II (*2 Tim.* 1:8-10). The Greek word *sumbolon* is used.

Christ did and speaking the words that he spoke."[1]

The speaking of the eucharistic words of Christ, "This is my Body" and "This is my Blood," is of the greatest importance to St. Thomas Aquinas. He notes that in other Sacraments the priest speaks in his own person, using the first person singular: "I baptize," "I absolve," etc.;[2] however, at the Eucharist, the priest says, "This is my body," enacting the image of Christ. "But the form of this Sacrament," explains St. Thomas, "is pronounced as if Christ were speaking in person."[3] Later the "Angelic Doctor" explains that the dignity of the Eucharist requires that this Sacrament "is performed only as in the person of Christ (*in persona Christi*)."[4] In addition, St. Thomas says that the priest "bears Christ's image, in Whose person and by Whose power he pronounces the words of consecration."[5] St. Thomas's contemporary, St. Bonaventure, teaches, as already mentioned, that the priest "signifies Christ the Mediator."[6] In our own century, the Second Vatican Council echoes these Scholastic theologians when it describes the priest as one "who presides over the assembly in the person of Christ."[7]

---

[1]John Chrysostom, *On the Treachery of Judas*, 1.6.

[2]Examples of this in our Anglican Prayer-book tradition include: "I baptize thee . . ." (p. 537); "I absolve thee . . ." (p. 582); and "I anoint thee . . . " (p. 586). Even in the Declaration at a wedding, the priest says, "I pronounce that they be man [husband] and wife together. . ." (p. 567).

[3]Thomas Aquinas, *Summa Theologia*, III, q. 78, a. 1.

[4]*Ibid.*, III, q. 82, a. 1. St. Thomas continues: "Now whoever performs any act in the person of another must do so only by the power bestowed from that other. . . .the power of consecrating this sacrament on Christ's behalf is bestowed upon the priest at his ordination: for thereby he is put upon a level with them to whom the Lord said: *Do this for a commemoration of Me.*" In a subsequent article, the phrase *in persona Christi* is again used for the priest: "he consecrates as in the person of Christ" (q. 82., a. 3).

[5]*Ibid.*, III, q. 83, a. 1, ad 3.

[6]Bonaventure, *Commentarii in quatuor Libros Sententiarum Petri Lombardi*, d. 25, a. 2, q. 1. *Persona quae ordinatur significat Christum mediatorem.*

[7]*Sacrosanctum Concilium* (Constitution, 14 December, 1963), 33. The phrase *in persona Christi* appears often in Vatican II Documents. See also *Lumen Gentium* (Dogmatic Constitution, 21 November, 1964), 10 & 28; and *Presbyterorum Ordinis* (Decree, 7 December, 1965), 2 &13.

An Anglican Perspective

Many Anglican theologians have embraced the sacramental teaching of the celebrant as a representative of God the Father and God the Son. Archbishop Thomas Cranmer (1489-1556), architect of our Prayer Book, writes:

> The minister of the Church speaketh unto us God's own words, which we must take as spoken from God's own mouth, because that from his mouth it came, and his word it is, and not the minister's.[1]

George Herbert (1593-1633), in our most important Anglican work on pastoralia, says that the priest is a deputy in the place of Christ: a "priest may do that which Christ did, and by his authority, and as His Vicegerent."[2] Most succinctly, Fr. A. H. Baverstock says of the priest: "He *impersonates* Christ."[3]

This priestly representation at the Eucharist is more than an historical recollection of Jesus at the Last Supper. In consecrating and breaking the eucharistic bread, the priest also recalls our Lord's death on the cross. Archbishop Cranmer writes that when the priest

> ministereth to our sights Christ's holy sacraments, we must think Christ himself crucified and presented before our eyes, because the Sacraments so represent him, and be his sacraments, and not the priest's. . . as at the Lord's holy table the priest distributeth wine and bread to feed the body, so we must think that inwardly by faith we see Christ feeding both body and soul to eternal life.[4]

Charles Wheatly (1686-1742), in his study of the Prayer Book, says that in the words of Institution, "the priest performs to God the representative sacrifice of the death and passion of His Son."[5]

---

[1]Thomas Cranmer, *An Answer unto. . . Stephen Gardiner* (1551), V, 394, in *Writings and Disputations relative to the Sacrament of the Lord's Supper* (Parker Society: Cambridge University Press, 1844), p. 366.

[2]George Herbert, *A Priest to the Temple*, 1.

[3]A. H. Baverstock, *Priesthood in Liturgy and Life* (Faith Press, 1917), p. 31. The italics are the author's.

[4]Thomas Cranmer, *Op cit.*, V, 394.

[5]Charles Wheatly, *A Rational Illustration of the Book of Common Prayer* (Cambridge, 1858), p. 348.

The priest also signifies the High Priestly ministry of our Lord in heaven, the Risen and Ascended Christ, who has taken our humanity into the Godhead. Dr. Sparrow Simpson writes that the priest is "the visible representative at the altar of the invisible Consecrator, Jesus Christ."[1] Fr. A. G. Hebert, S.S.M. (1886-1962), reminds us that as we gather around the altar we are, "according to the real truth of things, assembled with angels and with saints round the altar on high at which the Lord Himself is the Priest. . . ."[2]

Therefore, the celebrant of the Eucharist makes a number of representations of Christ: the Son of God and Incarnate Word, the Institutor and Lord of the Eucharist, the Lord of Calvary, and our great High Priest, the Lord of Heaven.

"Natural Resemblance"

If the priest acts *in persona Christi*, then the priest should be a recognizable and perceptible sign of Christ the man. St. Thomas Aquinas teaches that "Sacramental signs represent what they signify by natural resemblance."[3] The Vatican Declaration, *Inter insigniores,* draws heavily on this passage in Aquinas:

There would not be this "natural resemblance" which must exist between Christ and his minister if the role were not taken by a man: in such a case it would be difficult to see in the minister the image of Christ. For Christ himself was and remains a man.[4]

Given her vast understanding of symbols, Dorothy Sayers (1893-1957) knew that a woman priest would not be satisfactory, neither in a theatrical nor a sacramental sense. She observes that a female priest "would be dramatically unsuitable since God, very sensibly, chose to be born as a man." She then remarks that

[1]W. J. Sparrow Simpson, *The Ministry and the Eucharist*, p. viii.

[2]A. G. Hebert, "Ministerial Episcopacy," in K. E. Kirk, *The Apostolic Ministry,* p. 521.

[3]Thomas Aquinas, *Scriptum super Libros Sententiarum Magistri Petri Lombardi,* IV, d. 25, q. 2, ad 4.

[4]Sacred Congregation for the Doctrine of the Faith, *Inter insigniores* ("On the Question of the Admission of Women to the Ministerial Priesthood," 1976), 5.3.

a female priest "is rather like Sarah Bernhardt playing Hamlet."[1] The "natural resemblance" would be missing. A female priest could not, in the unforgettable phrase of Dr. Austin Farrer (1904-68), be a "walking sacrament" of Christ.[2]

Bishop Robert Terwilliger (1917-1991), in his insightful tract on the ordination of women, speaks of the bishop or priest as "a sacramental sign." The Holy Spirit empowers the bishop or priest to be a symbolic representation, an outward and visible image of Christ, to continue sacramentally the ministry of Christ. "And the image," says Bishop Terwilliger, "must be right. He must be a man."[3] Dr. Terwilliger admits that he is drawing upon the rich and powerful tradition of the Orthodox Church, which clearly understands the priest as an icon of Christ, a sign of His presence.

The Priest as Icon

The 1988 Inter-Orthodox Consultation on Women, held at Rhodes, Greece, states that

in the typology of worship the unbroken tradition of the Church, with no exception at all, has called upon only certain men to serve at the Altar as Priests who iconically present to the Body of Christ her head and Lord, the High Priest Jesus Christ.[4]

It must be noted that the iconic role of the priest is not vague or fuzzy, not ethereal or Docetic, not just a loose idea of Christ, not merely "Christ the human being" or Christ "the Generic Person," but Christ the Son of God, incarnated as a man. An Orthodox

[1]Dorothy Sayers, in a private letter, cited by V. A. Demant, "Why the Christian Priesthood is Male," in *Women and Holy Orders* - Report of the Archbishops' Commission (Church Information Office, 1966), p. 113. Dr. Demant's essay has been published as a tract by the Church Literature Association (1977).

[2]Austin Farrer, "Walking Sacraments," in *A Celebration of Faith* (Hodder and Stoughton, 1970), p. 109. "The man who bears the Sacrament," says Farrer, "is sacramental himself; he is, one might almost say, himself a walking sacrament." According to Farrer, "there is a moment when the priest steps into the place of Christ himself, to do what Christ did, to bless and to break, to present the mysterious sacrifice before God Almighty" (p. 110).

[3]Robert E. Terwilliger, *Ordination of Men in Theological Perspective,* p. 21.

[4]*On the place of the Woman in the Orthodox Church and the Question of the Ordination of Women* (Rhodes, 1988), 5.3.

81

theologian, Fr. Thomas Hopko, writes:

> The sacramental priest is not the image of God or divinity in general. He is certainly not the image of the Trinity or of the Holy Spirit. He is the image of Jesus Christ, who makes known the Father in the Spirit within the life of God's Church. And this image can only be actualized and effected by certain male members of the Church, who are called and equipped for this ministry.[1]

St. Theodore of Studios (759-826) explains that the priest blesses with the sign of the cross rather than with an icon of Christ because the priest is himself an icon of Christ: "Standing before God and men, the priest in his priestly invocations is the representation of Christ."[2] It should be pointed out that this statement was written in the heat of the Iconoclastic Controversy (725-832). The iconoclasts (Gk. for "image-breakers") opposed the veneration of icons. Since they believed that only the human nature, and not the divine nature, of Jesus could be depicted in art, no artistic representation could be a truthful portrayal of the Christ. The emphasis the iconoclasts placed on Christ as a universal, and not a particular, man, contains a "subtle Docetism." However, the Doctrine of the Incarnation teaches us that Christ was not just an abstract or universal human being but a concrete, individual man. This means, of course, that the particularity of His male sexuality was, and is, significant. The iconic representation of Christ as a male, both in religious art and in His sacramental priests, is an important and truthful one.[3]

Can a woman priest be a true icon of Christ the Incarnate Son

[1] Thomas Hopko, "Women and the Priesthood: Reflections on the Debate," in *Women and the Priesthood*, ed. Thomas Hopko (St. Vladimir's, 1983), p. 184.

[2] Theodore Studite, *Seven Chapters against the Iconoclasts*, 4.

[3] There are, I believe, a number of theological connections to be discerned here, especially in regard to my earlier references to Gnosticism and Docetism. A good introduction to the Iconoclastic Controversy and some of the deeper theological issues involved will be found in Roman Cholij, "Considerations from the Eastern Churches," in *Man, Woman & Priesthood*, ed. J. Tolhurst, pp. 106-116. The phrase "subtle Docetism" is Fr. Cholij's (p. 111).

of God? Can she represent the Lord (not the Lady) of the Church? Can she image the Bridegroom (not the Bride) of His Church? Can she be a "walking sacrament" of Christ our High Priest? Can she be a "natural resemblance" of the male Christ? Can she be an effective, obvious, and practical sign of whom she represents?

In his recent *Letter to Women* (1995), Pope John Paul II points out that the sacramental or iconic role of male priests as shepherd and bridegroom is not "an arbitrary imposition" but God's own order, and "in no way detracts from the role of women" or even from the role of unordained males. "These role distinctions," says the Pontiff,

> should not be viewed in accordance with the criteria of functionality typical in human societies. Rather they must be understood according to the particular criteria of the *sacramental economy*, i.e. the economy of "signs" which God freely chooses in order to become present in the midst of humanity.[1]

The Sacraments, you see, are God's; and their immutable signs and conditions are His also.

[1]*Letter of Pope John Paul II to Women* (29 June, 1995), p. 21. This document should not to be confused with his Apostolic Letter, *Mulieris Dignitatem* ("On the Dignity and Vocation of Women," 1988).

4. Christian Unity

Oneness in Christ

On the night before He was betrayed, our Blessed Lord prayed for the unity of the Church: "that they all may be one; as thou Father, art in me, and I in thee; that they also may be one in us" (*Jn.* 17:21). Christian Unity was important for Him, and must be for us too. It is our duty to pray and work for the unity of Christendom, being careful to safeguard what unity we have, not to take it for granted, and not to erect new barriers. We earnestly pray: "Regard not our sins, but the faith of thy Church, and grant unto it that peace and unity which is agreeable to thy will."[1]

The specific relationship between Holy Orders and the unity of the Church is nothing new and nothing unique to Anglicanism. Commonly recognized Orders have always played a critical role in safeguarding the unity of the Church. In his standard work on sacramental theology, Canon Oliver Quick writes of this historical interdependence: "Recognized validity of Orders in bishops and priests was the link whereby the body of the Church was held together."[2] Likewise, Dr. Austin Farrer says of the priest: "He is the appointed flag for Christ's people to rally round: the centre of unity to which we hold in every place."[3]

Only a pathologically shy ostrich, with its head permanently planted in the ground, could believe that the ordination of women has not dissolved the link, not lowered the flag, and not dealt a severe blow to Christian Unity, both within the Anglican Communion and in our ecumenical relations with other churches.

[1]*Book of Common Prayer*, pp. 40 & 123.
[2]O. C. Quick, *The Christian Sacraments* (Nisbet, 1927), p. 140.
[3]Austin Farrer, "Walking Sacraments," *A Celebration of Faith,* p. 109.

The Anglican Communion

About half of the national churches of the Anglican Communion have proceeded with the ordination of women to the priesthood, causing division and tension in the worldwide communion between those provinces that have women priests and those that do not. Some of the provinces and dioceses that do not ordain women are reasonably confident that they will not fall prey to what is often perceived as a cultural phenomenon, a trend prevalent in the western, industrialized nations.

Those Churches which have ordained women have had their own problems: internal divisions, schisms, and mass exodus. The Episcopal Church in the United States has lost over a million members. I do not wish to imply that all million have left because of the ordination of women. Certainly other factors have contributed to this exodus. On the other hand, it is interesting to note that the ordination of women has not attracted great numbers to replace those who have left, for whatever reasons.

The ordination of women has led to the formation of several Continuing Anglican Churches, which in a relatively short time can boast almost 1,000 congregations. These continuing bodies are fully authentic Anglican churches, which continue to be loyal to the Scriptures and Tradition of the Church Catholic, which use *the Book of Common Prayer*, which uphold the threefold Apostolic Ministry, and therefore, which do not ordain women. In addition, a significant number of individuals, both clergy and laity, have left the Anglican Family altogether and have found new spiritual homes in the Roman Catholic or Orthodox Churches.

All of us have dear friends who, in good conscience, have made difficult, heart-wrenching decisions about moving to new ecclesial homes. I have enormous respect for all these people and keep them in my prayers. The Anglican Church has been greatly impoverished by the departure of these highly principled people, generally men and women of strong catholic conviction, and, obviously, of great integrity. Consequently, I fear that

Anglicanism is in very grave danger of losing its theological balance. "Liberal Catholics" do not, and can not, provide the Catholic perspective necessary for a healthy Anglican balance.

Others have opted, at least for the present moment, to stay in the Anglican Communion, despite her brokenness and disarray. These so-called Traditionalists see themselves as a faithful remnant within a fractured, tension-filled, and extremely polarized Anglican Church. Amidst all the unrest, pettiness, discrimination, persecution, and unseemly court battles, they seek to remain faithful to Scripture and the Apostolic Tradition.

Impaired Communion

Tragically the Anglican Church no longer has a commonly recognized ministry nor commonly recognized Sacraments. Provinces, dioceses, parishes, congregations, religious orders, and households have been split over the issue of women's ordination. Many of us in good conscience cannot, and will not, receive sacramental administrations from women priests. This sorry situation is what the 1988 Lambeth Conference refers to as "impaired" communion.[1] The Eames Commission employs this same terminology for what it calls the "actual diminishment of the degree of communion." The Commission also suggests the possibility of other terminology such as "restricted" or "incomplete communion." "In either case" says the Report, "communion is less full than it was."[2]

We are no longer in full sacramental communion or full eucharistic fellowship, not within our own worldwide Anglican family, not even within our own national churches, provinces, dioceses, and parishes. There now exists in the Anglican Church, side by side, what the Church of England, including the Archbishop of Canterbury, refers to as "two integrities," those who accept the ordination of women and those who do not. Many lay people, both women and men, are firmly opposed to

[1]*The Truth Shall Make You Free: The Lambeth Conference 1988* (Church House, 1988), Resolution 1.2 (p. 201).
[2]Eames Commission, *Report* (1989), ¶44, p. 21.

87

the ordination of women, but sometimes impairment is felt most acutely in the priesthood itself. Among the clergy, there no longer can be mutual recognition and acceptance of one another's orders. The college of presbyters has indeed been fractured and can no longer gather as a common ministerial priesthood, not at ordination services, not even on Maundy Thursday.[1]

Bishop Charles Gore writes of the historical and binding relationship between the bishop and his college of priests: "They are his recognized council, advisors, co-operators; he does nothing without them."[2] The Prayer-book Ordinal makes this collegial relationship crystal clear by directing that "the Bishop with the Priests present shall lay their hands severally upon the head of every one that receives the Order of Priesthood."[3] St. Paul mentions this "laying on of the hands of the presbytery" (*1 Tim.* 4:14), as do many of the ancient liturgical rites.[4] With the advent of women's ordination, this presbyteral sharing, this priestly collegiality, is no longer possible. And there are grave theological consequences. As Dom Gregory Dix states: "A single presbyter, apart from his fellows, has really no meaning."[5]

Unity in Diversity?
History shows us that the Anglican Church has not always been kind to those who do not take the official party line. The Church of England's treatment of Roman Catholics and Non-

[1]It is a venerable custom for the priests of a diocese to gather with their bishop at the Chrismal Mass (blessing of holy oils), celebrated by him on Maundy Thursday, usually in the cathedral church.

[2]Charles Gore, *Christian Ministry*, p. 168.

[3]*Book of Common Prayer*, p. 655.

[4]The *Apostolic Tradition,* the oldest surviving ordination liturgy, explains that the priest does not ordain, but still has a significant part to play: "he rather is to put his seal on the ordination of a presbyter while the bishop ordains." In this early liturgy the new priest is invited to "share in the presbyterate." The ancient ordination prayers of Rome ask that the new priests may be "virtuous colleagues of our order." In the Spanish rite of ordination, the new priest is greeted with these words: "Behold, brother, thou hast become a colleague of our order." For other examples, see H. B. Porter, *The Ordination Prayers of the Ancient Western Churches* (SPCK, 1967).

[5]Gregory Dix, *Holy Order,* p. 19.

Conformists, not to mention the persecution of her own Ritualists, are not among our proudest Anglican moments. But generally, the Anglican Communion has long been considered a roomy, spacious, and comprehensive church, which encourages diversity and accommodates wide differences, which is able to live with loose ends and some degree of untidiness, which respects the individual's freedom of conscience, which is gracious to its minorities and certainly not afraid of including them. Great diversity is permitted in nonessentials, matters that are sometimes called *adiaphora* (Gk. for "things indifferent"). For example, the Thirty-nine Articles are, according to Dr. Peter Toon, "minimal in their requirements, leaving many secondary questions open."[1] They provide Anglicans with what Dr. Oliver O'Donovan styles a "characteristic manouverability."[2]

But I have been describing classical Anglicanism, not current practice. Unfortunately, there is now at work in Anglicanism a narrowness, smallness, and mean-spiritedness, which is not respectful of differences or tolerant of minorities and which seeks to exclude, rather than to include. I am sorry to say that much of this has come about, or at least been greatly intensified, through the ordination of women. In many parts of the Anglican Communion, a difficult situation has frequently been compounded by those who try to impose their personal acceptance of women priests on others. On the whole, these heavy-handed, so-called "liberal" Anglicans continue to pay lip-service to inclusivity, and talk *ad nauseam* about "unity in diversity," "our diocesan family," "collegiality," and so forth, while their exclusive, discriminatory, and petty actions render such language empty and meaningless, "as sounding brass, or a tinkling cymbal."

---

[1]Peter Toon, "The Articles and Homilies," in *The Study of Anglicanism,* ed. Stephen Sykes and John Booty (SPCK, 1988). p. 136.

[2]Oliver O'Donovan, *On the Thirty Nine Articles: A Conversation with Tudor Christianity* (Paternoster, 1986), p. 104. Also see my paper, "Catholic and Reformed: the Idea of the Church in the Elizabethan Settlement," in *The Idea of the Church in Historical Development*, ed. D. A. Petley (St. Peter Publications, 1995), especially pp. 31-33.

Again and again, the "liberal" majority presently in control has demonstrated just how threatened and insecure it is in its new, synod-forged faith and how little tolerance it can muster for even the tiniest pocket of resistance. Promises and assurances made to Traditionalists that there would still be room for them once women were ordained have been broken. In Canada, for example, the 1986 General Synod revoked the conscience clause protecting those who still affirm the biblical teaching of an all-male Apostolic Ministry. Of course, such a synodical act did not revoke conscience itself; and many people of good conscience, including many young people, continue to respond to God's call to accept and uphold His divine order, not the order of General Synod. Such obedience can be costly.

One hears many sad stories of intolerance and persecution. It is ironic that a Church which speaks so often about reaching out to the "marginalized" in our society has deliberately marginalized loyal members of its own family. Life-long, faithful Anglicans are often made to feel like strangers in their own Church. Outstanding young male candidates -- bright, well-educated and holy men -- who in good conscience cannot accept the ordination of women are often refused ordination. Traditionalist priests, however senior and esteemed, are rarely appointed honorary canons. Massive campaigns are launched to stop traditionalist bishops from being elected or ratified. All this, of course, is remarkably petty, utterly shameful, and extremely un-Anglican.

It is grossly absurd that such a huge effort is expended on making a recent innovation, a practice unknown in the Church for nearly 2,000 years, the one belief mandatory for ordination and preferment. How can a novelty, of only a few years' standing, with no support in Scripture or Tradition, suddenly be the one required doctrine of the Anglican Church, the sole basis of inclusion or exclusion? People may be ordained priest or even consecrated bishop if they question the resurrection of Christ, endorse same-sex marriages, and openly engage in things that should not even be done "in secret" (*Eph.* 5:12), but not if they take St. Paul's biblical position on women's ordination.

How much longer this kind of foolishness, intolerance, and injustice will be endured remains to be seen. Even the most forbearing of Traditionalists have their breaking point. More and more I sense that if new accommodations and safeguards for Traditionalists, including new provincial structures, are disallowed, large-scale schism may be the only way of preserving classical Anglicanism. And so the harm which the ordination of women has caused the Anglican Communion cannot be understated. The damage is severe, and some fear irreparable. We are only beginning to discover the terrible discord and the depths of pain and distrust the ordination of women has caused, and we cannot possibly grasp the long-term implications.

The Ecumenical Scene

The Anglican Communion is so broken by the ordination of women and other controversial matters that it has not been able to pursue reunion with other churches as vigorously as it once did. Yet I must I say something about the larger picture.

The Greek word *oikouméne* literally means "the whole inhabited world." In other words, ecumenism does not pertain to a narrow, sectarian view but demands a wide, Catholic, world view. And so we must ask: Is there an ecumenical perspective on the ordination of women?

If we survey all of Christendom, we discover a diversity of practice in regard to the ordination of women. Most of the liberal, "mainline" Protestant churches ordain women. However, the more conservative Protestant denominations, such as the Southern Baptist Church, the largest Protestant body in the United States, the Lutheran Church, Missouri Synod, and the Free Presbyterian Church of Scotland, do not ordain women on the basis of the teaching of Holy Scripture.

When we look to the Catholic churches, that is, the Roman Catholic Church and the Eastern Orthodox Churches (the ancient Greek and Russian churches), the Oriental Orthodox Churches, and the Old Catholic Church (including the [Polish] National

Catholic Church) -- which all together comprise at least three-quarters of Christendom -- we find a general consensus which upholds the view of Scripture and Tradition heretofore presented. This Catholic perspective ought to be of great importance to Anglicans, who claim that their ministry and Sacraments are not at variance with those of the Church Catholic.

Anglicans and Catholic Christendom

Anglicans have always maintained that they are not the entire Church Catholic but a legitimate part, however small, of the same. The Anglican Church, in Evelyn Underhill's memorable phrase, is "a respectable suburb of the city of God -- but all the same, part of 'greater London.'"[1] Richard Hooker is adamant that at the Reformation the English Church did not sever itself from the Church Catholic: "In the Church we were, and we are so still."[2] But neither does he believe that Anglicans have any exclusive rights or claims to Catholicism, and he speaks of the Catholic Church being "divided into a number of distinct Societies."[3]

Until recently Anglicans have been reasonably humble about their place in the worldwide family of Catholic Churches. Numbers really should make them humble! Recent statistics show that Anglicans represent about three per cent (3%) of Christendom (Catholics and Protestants combined) and about five per cent (5%) of Catholic Christendom. Anglicans are small fish in a gigantic pond! It would be anything but humble for such a small part of Catholic Christendom to believe that it has some fundamental understanding of Catholic Sacraments and Orders which the rest of Catholic Christendom lacks.

What do the Catholic Churches officially teach?

It is important for us to hear what our Catholic relatives are

[1]Evelyn Underhill, in a letter to Dom John Chapman (9 June, 1931), in *The Letters of Evelyn Underhill*, ed. Charles Williams (Longmans, Green, & Co., 1943), p. 195.
[2]Richard Hooker, *Of the Laws of Ecclesiastical Polity*, III.10.1.
[3]*Ibid.*, III.1.14.

saying about this matter. The Roman Catholic Church, at its highest levels, has most consistently and emphatically stated its objection to the ordination of women. Pope John Paul II, in his Apostolic Letter, *Ordinatio Sacerdotalis*, states: "I declare that the Church has no authority whatsoever to confer priestly ordination on women and that this judgment is to be definitively held by all the Church's faithful."[1] To avoid any misunderstanding about the official and binding nature of this papal pronouncement, Joseph Cardinal Ratzinger, Prefect of the Congregation for the Doctrine of the Faith, has, with the Pope's permission, further explained that this statement is "a matter of full definitive assent, that is to say, irrevocable, to a doctrine taught infallibly by the Church."[2] Such definitive teaching can not, and will not, be easily overturned.

Likewise the Orthodox Churches have consistently voiced their fundamental objection to the ordination of women. At the 1978 Anglican-Orthodox gathering in Athens, the Orthodox stated: "The ordination of women to the priesthood is an innovation, lacking any basis whatever in Holy Tradition."[3] Furthermore, they declared that they did not see such ordinations as part of "the creative continuity of Tradition" but as "a violation of the apostolic faith and order of the Church."[4] According to the 1984 Dublin Statement: "The Orthodox affirm that such ordination is impossible, since it is contrary to Scripture and tradition."[5] The Orthodox position was reaffirmed by the 1988 inter-orthodox consultation held in Rhodes, which speaks of "the impossibility of the ordination of women to the special priesthood as founded in the tradition of the Church."[6] This

[1] John Paul II, *Ordinatio Sacerdotalis* (Pentecost, 22 May, 1994), 4.
[2] Joseph Cardinal Ratzinger, *Responsum* (28 October, 1995).
[3] The Anglican-Orthodox Joint Doctrinal Commission, *The Athens Report* (1978), III.3.
[4] *Ibid.*, III.4.
[5] *Anglican-Orthodox Dialogue: The Dublin Agreed Statement* (1984), IV. 103. The section continues: "With this some Anglicans agree, while others believe that it is possible, and even desirable. . . ."
[6] *On the Place of the Woman in the Orthodox Church and the Question of the Ordination of Women* (1988), I.4.

view has also been eloquently expressed in the writings of eminent Orthodox theologians, such as Bishop Kallistos Ware and Fathers Alexander Schmemann, Thomas Hopko, and Roman Cholij.

The Ecumenical Implications

Given the firm and consistent teaching of the great Catholic Churches on the ordination of women, there are serious ecumenical risks in the Anglican Church going its separate way in this matter and acting *ultra vires*, that is beyond its power and authority.

Rome has repeatedly warned that the ordination of women by Anglicans will have major ecumenical consequences. Pope Paul VI, in a letter to Archbishop Donald Coggan, spoke of the ordination of women as "so grave a new obstacle and threat" to reconciliation.[1] Pope John Paul II wrote to Archbishop Robert Runcie that the ordination of women "constitutes, in the eyes of the Catholic Church, an increasingly serious obstacle."[2] Johannes Cardinal Willebrands, Head of the Vatican Secretariat for Christian Unity, wrote to Dr. Runcie that "a development like the ordination of women does nothing to deepen the communion between us and weakens the communion that currently exists."[3] The Common Declaration signed by Pope John Paul II and Archbishop George Carey, on December, 1996, in Rome, states: "The obstacle to reconciliation caused by the ordination of women as priests and bishops in some provinces of the Anglican Communion has also become increasingly evident, creating a new situation."[4] In his homily at the service in which the Declaration was signed, the Pope also mentioned the Church's "disagreement about conferring priestly ordination on women."[5]

[1]Letter of Pope Paul VI to the Archbishop of Canterbury, 23 March, 1976.

[2]Letter of Pope John Paul II to the Archbishop of Canterbury, 20 December, 1984.

[3]Letter of Johannes Cardinal Willebrands to the Archbishop of Canterbury, 17 June, 1986.

[4]Pope John Paul II, quoted in *the Church Times*, 13 December, 1996, p. 5.

[5]*Ibid.*, p. 8.

At the 1976 Anglican-Orthodox Conference at Moscow, the Orthodox members firmly warned: "If the Anglican Churches proceed to the ordination of women to the priesthood and episcopate, this will create a very serious obstacle to the development of our relations in the future."[1] In 1978 the Orthodox said: "If the Anglicans continue to ordain women to the priesthood, this will have a decisively negative effect on the issue of the recognition of Anglican orders."[2] The report said that by ordaining women, Anglicans "would sever themselves from this continuity," that is, from the Apostolic Succession.[3]

Despite such clear-cut warnings, Anglicans have persisted in their own private agenda, shown little or no restraint, and have taken unilateral action, thereby seriously jeopardizing the unity of the Church. Anglicans, who once liked to describe themselves as "the bridge church," linking the Catholic and Reformed worlds, have been intent on closing, disconnecting, and even burning their bridges. This is most unfortunate, particularly given the great advances that had been made in ecumenical relations. Again I quote Canon John Macquarrie, speaking to the bishops at the 1978 Lambeth Conference: "We may be paying a very high price for what we are doing."[4]

Ecumenical Councils
Since Holy Orders are God's gift to the whole Church Catholic and not the possession of any one branch of Catholic

[1]Anglican-Orthodox Joint Doctrinal Commission, *The Moscow Agreed Statement*, (SPCK, 1976), p. 76. This resolution, passed at the Moscow meeting, is in the report, but is not part of the agreed statement. The resolution continues: "Although the Anglican members are divided among themselves on the theological principle involved, they recognize the strength of Orthodox convictions on this matter and undertake to make this known to their Churches."
[2]*The Athens Report* (1978), III.5. This portion of *the Athens Report* is also printed in *the Dublin Agreed Statement* (St. Vladimir's, 1985), p. 60.
[3]*Ibid.*
[4]John Macquarrie, at the 1978 Lambeth Conference (Hearing B, 31st July, 1978). This quotation appears in the abridged version of Dr. Macquarrie's remarks, printed in an Appendix of the 1978 Lambeth Report (Church Information Office, 1978), p. 119.

Christendom, it would take much more than a local synod to alter the historic ministry. No single church is competent to change such a universal Tradition. It would demand at least an Ecumenical Council, that is a synod of the whole Catholic Church, East and West. Evelyn Underhill said that chief among her many reasons for opposing the ordination of women was her belief that "so complete a break with Catholic tradition cannot be made save by the consent of a united Christendom." She then remarks: "Any local or national Church which makes it [the break] will drop at once to the level of an eccentric sect."[1] When the Church of England's General Synod voted for women priests in November, 1992, John Gummer, then England's Minister of Agriculture and a member of synod, announced his decision to leave the Anglican Church and become a Roman Catholic in these same sobering and prophetic terms: "In ordaining women, the Church of England becomes a sect, and I cannot therefore be a member of a sect."[2]

Alas, an Ecumenical Council, which could give the consent of a united Catholic Christendom, is not possible in our present circumstances, nor in the foreseeable future. However, the possibility for such a council must not be ruled out. Great ecumenical strides have been made between the Orthodox and Roman Churches in recent years and a new level of dialogue achieved. Anglicans must be careful lest they be left out in the cold, all alone, "an eccentric sect."

Of course, even if an Ecumenical Council could be convened, many of us believe that it would not have the authority to overturn Scripture and Tradition in this matter. Councils, even of an ecumenical nature, are not infallible, as the Church herself is not infallible.[3] As Article XXI states, councils "may err,

---

[1] Evelyn Underhill, "The Ideals of the Ministry of Women," in *Mixed Pasture* (London, 1933), p. 113.

[2] Reported in *The Christian Challenge*, XXXI, 9 (December, 1992), p. 8.

[3] The Church is not infallible in that she is very capable of being led astray and of making mistakes, and indeed has made many. The Church, however, is indefectible, that is, she cannot forever fall into error and cannot completely

and sometimes have erred, even in things pertaining unto God."[1] If this be true of great councils, how true it must be of local or national synods. Sadly, however, one encounters Anglicans who feel that their own puny synods are somehow infallible!

Reception

Even if a duly qualified Ecumenical Council were to come to a common mind on some doctrinal issue, the process does not stop there. Synods of the highest order can not only be mistaken but can be unrepresentative of the larger church. Their decisions can become more and more disunifying. Therefore, synodical decisions must be received by the whole Church, must demonstrate their continuity and lasting power. Dr. E. J. Bicknell (1882-1934) writes:

> The decrees of even the largest and most representative council are not the Church's last word on the subject . . . they need to be ratified by the general acceptance of the Church at large, not necessarily at the moment but after consideration.[2]

The degree of acceptance or reception must be tested widely, over a long period of time.

Gamaliel's Principle

In Anglican circles, reception is often spoken of as "Gamaliel's principle," a reference to the opinion of a certain Gamaliel, a "doctor of the law" mentioned in *Acts*. Gamaliel teaches: "If this counsel or this work be of men, it will come to nought: But if it be of God, ye cannot overthrow it" (5:38-39). Many Anglicans have adopted this concept in dealing with controversial matters like the ordination of women. A disputed matter is adopted tentatively and then must be accepted or

fail. Christ promised that "the gates of hell shall not prevail against" His Church (*Mt.* 16:18), and that He would be with the Church "even unto the end of the world" (*Mt.* 28:20). The indefectibility of the Church does not rule out numerous errors, false starts, and wrong turns.

[1]*Book of Common Prayer*, pp. 706-7. Likewise, Article XIX states: "As the Church of Jerusalem, Alexandria, and Antioch, have erred; so also the Church of Rome hath erred, not only in their living and manner of Ceremonies, but also in matters of Faith" (p. 706).

[2]E. J. Bicknell, *The Thirty-Nine Articles*, p. 272.

rejected, must be allowed either to flourish or to lose support and disappear. The 1988 Lambeth Report upholds this process of reception, noting that an issue "continues to be tested until it is clearly accepted or not accepted by the whole Church."[1] This can be a very dangerous principle as it can involve giving people something which, even in small doses, may not be good for them. A little poison can be deadly! However, if one does believe at all in reception or the "Gamaliel principle," then that process must be genuinely allowed to operate.

Obviously, given the present state of unrest in Anglicanism, reception of the ordination of women has not yet occurred, and it may not occur. There is a great tentativeness about the ordination of women, both in the Anglican Communion and in the Church Universal. The English House of Bishops has reported:

> Even if the reception process is completed by the Church of England, the decision still has to be accepted by the entire Anglican Communion and indeed by the universal Church before it can be deemed to be the mind of Christ for his Church.[2]

The Eames Commission speaks of "accepting a degree of provisionality" in regard to the decision-making process about women priests and bishops.[3] The Commission cautions: "The fact that a synod has reached a decision does not foreclose the matter." Both proponents and opponents of women's ordination are urged to "be as open as possible, recognizing that synodical decisions may indeed come to be overwhelmingly affirmed, or, on the other hand, equally as overwhelmingly rejected."[4]

Reception or Coercion?
Reception cannot be forced by pressure tactics but can only

[1] "Mission and Ministry Report," 133, in *The Truth Shall Make You Free: The Lambeth Conference 1988*, p. 58.
[2] *The Ordination of Women to the Priesthood* - A Second Report by the House of Bishops (Church House, 1988), ¶177, p. 109.
[3] Eames Commission, *Report* (Church House, 1989), ¶21, p. 13; also see ¶33, p. 17. Part II of the Report (Church House, 1990) clarifies that the provisionality is "about the development itself" (6.1, p. 12).
[4] *Ibid.* (1989), ¶31, p. 16.

take place freely, openly, and honestly. In the words of the 1938 Doctrine Report, cited on p. 55, consensus must be "genuinely free." The Report again cautions that "great regard should be paid to the need for securing a free consensus, as distinct from an enforced uniformity."[1] True reception or free consensus can never be coerced.

The English House of Bishops emphasize that "sensitivity to those who remain opposed is essential" and that "care needs to be expressed through detailed safeguards to ensure that people are not forced to accept the administrations of a woman against their conscience."[2] The Eames Commission points out that "dissent should not be marginalized or excluded."[3] The Commission says:

> Bishops and dioceses who accept and endorse the ordination of women to the priesthood and episcopate would need to recognize, that within a genuinely open process of reception, there must still be room for those who disagree.[4]

Bishop Michael Nazir-Ali, one of the co-secretaries of the Eames Commission, has sensibly argued that in the process of reception,

> every effort should be made to see that those who dissent from whatever decision has been made are not excluded from the life of the Church and its decision-making bodies. Only in this way can reception be genuine.[5]

The Joint Meeting of the Anglican Primates and the Anglican Consultative Council (Cape Town, 1993) states in Resolution 14, that it "reaffirms the continuing place in the Anglican Communion both of those who oppose and those who accept the ordination of women." Furthermore, the Resolution calls upon all Anglican bishops "to be scrupulously fair in the exercise of pastoral care to those who oppose and those who accept the ordination of women, particularly those who are in minority

---

[1] *Doctrine in the Church of England* (1938), p. 39.
[2] *A Second Report* (1988), p. 109.
[3] Eames Commission, *Report* (1989), ¶ 31, p. 16.
[4] *Ibid.*, ¶42, p. 20.
[5] Michael Nazir-Ali, *Church Times*, 11 September, 1992.

situations."[1] Such fairplay is essential if reception is to be given an honest chance.

Bishops and Dioceses that try to exclude Traditionalists from the Church's life -- for example, by not ordaining Traditionalist candidates -- are not acting in good faith and are not honouring the process of reception nor "Gamaliel's principle." In a heavy-handed and unfair way, they are trying to prejudice the outcome, to enforce uniformity, and to make consensus anything but "genuinely free." Such a prejudicial approach could have some short-term success for various causes and preoccupations of the day, but the long-term prognosis, both for specific dioceses and for the larger Church, cannot be good.

Ecumenical Frontiers

In spite of Anglicans' fragmentation and their unilateral and sectarian action in the matter of ordaining women, we must not lose heart and believe that all is forever lost ecumenically. There are very positive signs of hope. Provinces of the Anglican Church that do not ordain women, such as Papua New Guinea, are carrying on their own ecumenical talks with the Roman Catholic Church. Continuing Anglican Churches are also involved in conversations with the Roman Catholic Church and other Catholic Churches.

Dr. Graham Leonard, the former Anglican Bishop of London and now a Roman Catholic priest, was absolutely right when he talked about "a second Reformation," a massive realignment of Christendom, being underway.[2] In due course, Traditionalists

---

[1]*A Transforming Vision: Cape Town, 1993* - The Official Report of the Joint Meeting of the Primates of the Anglican Communion and the Anglican Consultative Council (Church House, 1993), Resolution 14.2,4, pp. 145-146.

[2]For example, see Dr. Leonard's "The Tyranny of Subjectivism" (43rd annual John Findley Green Foundation Lecture, 18 September, 1987, Westminster College, Fulton, Missouri). The basic realignment which Dr. Leonard outlines is between those "who believe that the Christian Gospel is revealed by God" and those who think that the Gospel "can and should be modified and adapted to the cultural and intellectual attitudes and demands of successive generations."

may greet this new Reformation and radical regrouping as a very positive, happy, and unifying development, made possible by the ordination of women and other divisive issues presently before us.

As we seek our Lord's will for His Church, we must be genuinely open to new possibilities, structures, and arrangements within Catholic Christendom. In this regard, a very great responsibility has been placed on Anglican Traditionalists. Let us pray that all Traditionalist Anglicans, both those who have remained in the old national churches of the Communion, and those who have formed the Continuum, will work together in a co-operative spirit. We should be greatly encouraged that Forward in Faith, the Traditionalist movement in the Church of England, has declared that it is in full communion with the Traditional Anglican Communion, the largest continuing church body. We should be encouraged that the Episcopal Synod of America (ESA) has recently expressed a desire to pursue inter-communion. Can we really do otherwise? For we share and hold fast the same Faith, Orders, and Sacraments.

Prayer and Holiness

The quest for Christian unity, which is not simply camaraderie nor "chumminess" but God's unity in truth, can never be separated from the life of prayer. We must pray for unity, as Christ Himself prayed. We must pray for those with whom we seriously disagree. We must pray for the Church Universal, in those unforgettable words of Archbishop William Laud (1573-1645): "where it is divided and rent asunder, make it whole again."[1]

In our search for God's truth and unity, we must, as I have stressed in this book, return to the teachings of Scripture and the Tradition of the Church. We must look to great teachers and theologians for deeper knowledge and understanding. We must also avail ourselves of the spiritual guidance of saintly men and women, those who demonstrate great holiness of life. Dr. E. J. Bicknell reminds us that "the experts in the Christian religion

[1]*Book of Common Prayer,* p. 39.

101

are the saints, not the theologians"; and he advises us that "if the opinions of the scholar or the theologian are inconsistent with the experience of the saint, we may rightly hesitate to adopt them." He continues: "The ascertainment of Christian truth calls for the effort of the whole man. It demands prayer no less than study. Spiritual vision is something deeper than intellectual vision."[1]

As we seek to be faithful to God's revelation in Scripture and the Tradition of the Church and true to our convictions, we must not despair or become demoralized; we must avoid cynicism, negativism, bitterness, and self-righteousness. Let us remain positive and cheerful; let us walk in the newness of life which God in Christ graciously offers us. Let us always be "speaking the truth in love" (*Eph*.4:15). Let us be a good witness to our own people and even to those who hate and persecute us, challenging the latter to be more tolerant and pastoral.

Let us be prepared to make sacrifices but not to waste valuable time and energy in useless fights, ill-conceived and fudging schemes, or foolish compromises. Let us put our energy into feeding Christ's sheep, teaching the Faith, fostering vocations to the ministry, building up our respective parishes and congregations, and safeguarding their unity. John Keble once said: "If the Church of England were to fail, it should be found in my parish."[2] This is not rabid congregationalism or isolationism but the sincere and honest desire of a great Catholic churchman to preserve all that is best, noblest, and most unifying in the Anglican tradition. Let us wholeheartedly commit ourselves to that blessèd task.

[1] E. J. Bicknell, *The Thirty-Nine Articles*, p. 274.
[2] John Keble, cited in Edmund Purcell, *Life of Cardinal Manning* (Macmillan, 1896), I, 529. Cardinal Manning recalls that the context of Keble's famous remark was the ruling of the Privy Council in the Gorham Trial (1850). Keble knew that whatever general apostasy occurred in the Church of England, the Catholic principles of that Church would still be found in his parish of Hursley, near Winchester, which he served from 1836 until his death in 1866. John R. Griffin comments on this remark: "I contend that Keble meant exactly what he said." *John Keble: Saint of Anglicanism* (Mercer University Press, 1987), p. 104.

5. Social and Political Issues

The Great Dividing-Line

For me, the ordination of women is primarily a matter of theology, not politics nor sociology. Therefore, in this book, I have been stressing theological arguments based on Scripture, Tradition, sacramental theology, and the unity of the Church. For me, truly compelling arguments about the ordination of women *must* be found in these places and not in secular politics or the latest social theories.

Many advocates of women's ordination, who see their cause as primarily a political or sociological one, would downplay or dismiss altogether the theological arguments. How often have synods or other church bodies been unwilling to consider the deeply theological nature of this question? How often have we been informed that there are *no* theological objections to the ordination of women? How often have we heard that justice for women is more important than what St. Paul says or more important than the unity of the Church? How often have we encountered crass forms of power politics, including excessive lobbying, character assassination, and forced and illegal ordinations, like the infamous one I attended in 1974 in Philadelphia?

These two approaches to the subject -- the biblical/theological and the social/political -- would seem radically opposed. And generally they are! More than twenty-five years ago Dr. Mascall pointed out that one's position on women's ordination really came down to where one stood in this regard:

> The real dividing line is between those who believe in the fundamentally revealed and given character of the Christian religion and those who find their norms in the outlooks and assumptions of contemporary secularised culture and are

103

concerned to assimilate the beliefs and institutions of Christianity to it.[1]

In a later essay, Dr. Mascall again writes about this fundamental choice:

. . . whether the Christian religion is something revealed by God through his incarnate Son, which places us under loyalty and obedience to him, or whether it is something which we have the right to make up to our own specifications, by democratic processes and majority votes, in accordance with our own desires and the pressures of contemporary society.[2]

This, I believe, is not a harsh or extreme appraisal, but a true understanding of the ever-widening division in today's Church: between those who believe in divine revelation and those who put their trust in a new brand of "Christianity," which has evolved from a malignant, obsessive concern with this world and an extreme politicalization of the Church and her Faith.

Many in the contemporary Church no longer define the Faith in light of Scripture or the Creeds or the following of the Apostles, but in terms of modern-day political and social values; they are more concerned with the ills of a transient, changing society than with the condition of the immortal souls which have been entrusted to the Church's care. Dr. Edward Norman, in the 1978 Reith Lectures, argued that Christianity today is

preoccupied with political and social change throughout the world. But Christianity today is also notable for its lack of a distinctly *Christian* attitude towards the world it wishes to see changed. It has increasingly borrowed its political outlook and vocabulary, the issues it regards as most urgently requiring attention, and even its tests of moral virtue, from the progressive thinking of the surrounding secular culture.[3]

[1]E. L. Mascall, *Women Priests?* (1972), p. 24.

[2]"Some Basic Considerations," in *Man, Woman, & Priesthood (1978)*, p. 26. Dr. Mascall's "dividing line" is also the basis of Dr. Graham Leonard's "realignment" or "second Reformation" theory, mentioned on p. 100.

[3]Edward Norman, *Christianity and the World Order* (Oxford University Press, 1979), p. 15. Also see *After the Deluge: Essays Towards the Desecularization of the Church*, ed. William Oddie (SPCK, 1987), and *Redeeming the Time: The Church and the Challenge of Secularity*, ed. David Garrett (St. Peter Publications, 1994).

His assessment, I believe, collaborates Dr. Mascall's thesis and goes to the heart of our contemporary dilemma.   Dr. Robert Crouse provides further collaboration: "But the world will not be saved by de-sacralising the saving Word.   Secularity is redeemed only by what is beyond the secular."[1]

Progress

Many advocates of women's ordination sincerely believe that humanity has made tremendous advances since Apostolic times and that we are much wiser than all who have gone before. Therefore, they believe that the Church must adapt to the new, progressive, politically-correct insights of our times, to new and better social values and to nobler ideologies.

The concept of progress is a difficult and many-faceted one. Surely there have been enormous advances in science and technology which assist us in our daily work and which affect the longevity and quality of life.   Surely there have been social changes which have improved the status of women, children, and various minorities and which have benefited the fabric of society. These are good and commendable developments, and I certainly would want to laud them.

However, not everything improves with age.   Not all "progress" is genuine progress.   When we look to the oppressive twentieth-century regimes in Nazi Germany or Bosnia, our views of political advancement must be questioned. When we ponder world poverty and hunger or the high rates of divorce, suicide, abortion and cohabitation in western society, we must seriously question ideas of social progress. How can we honestly believe that humanity has come of age in the twentieth century? How can our society, with all its selfishness, cruelty, instability, and disorder, provide us with an ideal pattern of Church life? How can we believe that fallen humanity is more enlightened or righteous in this century? How can we defend the rightness or wrongness of something simply by the passage of time?

[1]R. D. Crouse, "Redeeming Secularity," in *Redeeming the Time* (see preceding note), p. 81

To speak of progress in terms of better understanding or rational development is surely intellectual pride. For some to suggest that they have a superior knowledge, a better grasp of theology than our Lord and St. Paul, is reminiscent of the early Gnostics, who claimed to have a special *gnosis* or knowledge quite separate from that of the Apostolic Church. St. Irenaeus, for example, reports that early heretics, confronted with the Apostolic Tradition preserved by the Church, would claim "that they themselves are wiser not merely than the presbyters, but even than the Apostles, because they have discovered the undiluted truth."[1] The Gnostics have many descendants in our day, people convinced of the wrongness of Scripture and 2,000 years of Tradition and of the absolute rightness of their own "undiluted truth." Such a high degree of self-confidence may be commendable, but such prideful arrogance is another matter.

Real progress is made when men and women are obedient to God's eternal word. Real progress is made when there is humility and repentance and amendment of life. It is in this context that C. S. Lewis understands progress, which is about
> getting nearer to the place where you want to be. And if you have taken a wrong turning, then to go forward does not get you any nearer. If you are on the wrong road, progress means doing an about-turn and walking back to the right road; and in that case the man who turns back soonest is the most progressive man.[2]

Women's Ordination & Slavery

Advocates of the ordination of women often liken an all-male priesthood to the institution of slavery. Without question, slavery was a great social evil, and we can be grateful that church leaders like William Wilberforce (1759-1833) worked mightily for its abolition. However, it is important to recognize that slavery was a man-made institution, not something to be compared with God's created order. On the other hand, both human sexuality

[1]Irenaeus, *Adversus haereses*, III.2. Bishop John Jewel writes that Montanus and Marcion "used to say, when with a contempt they rejected the Holy Scriptures, that themselves knew many more and better things than either Christ or the Apostles ever knew" (*Apologia*, IV).

[2]C. S. Lewis, *Mere Christianity* (Macmillan, 1952), p. 22.

and the Apostolic Ministry are of divine origin, created by God Himself. Dr. Roger Beckwith has said it well: "what man has created, man can abolish, but he cannot abolish what God has created."[1]

As explained on p. 12, sexual differentiation is good because it is pre-lapsarian, part of God's perfect creation prior to the fall. In marked contrast, slavery is one of the many aspects of our fallen human condition. As St. Basil the Great (c. 330-79) said, "Among men no one is a slave by nature."[2] This explains why great writers of the Christian Church have consistently spoken out against slavery as an evil, but why none have spoken out against the divine order of *Genesis* or Christ's ordering of His Church. God's creation is good, not evil. We dare not question the goodness of God and of His divinely-appointed gifts.

Justice and Human Rights

The abolition of slavery is not the only advancement made in human rights and the establishment of a more just society. In recent years women have assumed full and equal roles in the work place, in the professions, and society at large. Many believe that this egalitarianism should be reflected in the Church's ordained ministry. They often argue that women have a right to be bishops and priests, just as they have a right to be lawyers, doctors, soldiers, or whatever. Anything less, they argue, is male chauvinism, prejudice, patriarchy, and sexual oppression.

I find it difficult to believe that Jesus, the great friend and liberator of women, would perpetrate so great an injustice against women. Surely Christ, who is just and who justifies us, should not be accused of unfair discrimination in ordering His Church with a male Apostolic Ministry.

Today there seems to be general confusion and murkiness in distinguishing between the Christian religion and human rights

[1] Roger Beckwith, cited in Michael Harper, *Equal and Different*, p. 51.
[2] Basil, *De Spiritu Sancto (On the Holy Spirit)*, 20.51.

movements and legislation. More and more the Church embraces and canonizes the standards of secular or pagan culture as though they were the absolute truths of the Gospel. The inscrutable will of God is confused with the shifting mores and "trendy" platforms of contemporary society.   Dr. Edward Norman summarizes this tendency well:

> The Human Rights movement also provides the content of much of the present politicalization of Christianity. It identifies the Church with the moral sanctions claimed as the justification for the goals of western liberalism -- whose transient moral enthusiasms are, in characteristic bourgeois manner, represented as eternal verities. The aims of Human Rights campaigns are being given the authority of the laws of God.[1]

Life in Christ, however, is not about civil rights or anything that can be earned or merited but about divine justice and grace, which is entirely dependent on God's will.   In the Parable of the labourers in the vineyard, the God of Grace is not constrained by human rights legislation or fair business and compensation guidelines; instead, He pays every labourer, including those who came in the eleventh hour, the same wage.   When the other labourers complain about their rights, the householder [God] replies: "Is it not lawful for me to do what I will with mine own?" (*Mt.* 20:15).

Dr. Caroline Moore, a Fellow of Peterhouse, Cambridge, and defender of male priesthood, says that we must face "the humbling possibility that God's standards may not be self-evidently identical to ours." She argues that the civil laws upon which governments are built are

> manifestly good and right, as far as they go. But they do not go all the way to the Kingdom of Heaven. Reason alone cannot discover the means of salvation, which depends upon the law of grace, revealed by Christ.[2]

The ordained ministry is certainly not founded on civil laws,

---

[1]Edward Norman, *Christianity and the World Order*, p. 33.

[2]Caroline Moore, writing in *The Daily Telegraph*. Cited in *The Christian Challenge*, XXIX, 9 (December, 1990), p. 15.

but on God's justice, on His revealed law. Therefore, from beginning to end, the ministry is about grace. "But the whole action," says Jeremy Taylor, "being but a ministry, is a declaration of the effect and grace of God's vouchsafing."[1] The ministry is not simply another secular profession, a mere "nine to five" job, requiring collective bargaining units, equal rights legislation, and affirmative action programmes. It is a sacred vocation, a spiritual calling, a setting apart by God, according to His rules, not ours.

The ordained ministry, as indeed every vocation in our Lord's kingdom, does require the fulfilment of certain duties and obligations to God. It demands faithful and generous service, not the attainment of legal rights, privileges, or positions of power. Christ, who washed the Apostles' feet the night before He died on the cross, also charged: "Whosoever will come after me, let him deny himself, and take up his cross, and follow me" (*Mk*. 8:34; see also *Mt*. 16:24 & *Lk*. 9:23).   Christ, who said of Himself: "I receive not honour from men" (*Jn*. 5:41), does not call His ministers to earthly honours and dignities, not to worldly rights and equities, but to humble and obedient service. "Nor of men sought we glory," declares St. Paul (*1 Thess*. 2:6). St. John Chrysostom preaches: "True honour consists in neglecting honour, in making no account of it, but in saying and doing everything according to what seems good to God."[2]

Liberation Theology

Not all supporters of women's ordination are ardent feminists or zealous supporters of Women's Lib, but many, nevertheless, have been powerfully influenced by the feminist movement. It would be exceptionally naïve not to see that there is a connection between the ordination of women and feminist or liberation theology, which decries patriarchal language and institutions, which seeks to overturn God's revealed order, to discard biblical images of creation and redemption, and to repudiate images of God's fatherhood and Christ's Sonship. Is there a

[1]Jeremy Taylor, *Of the Office Ministerial*, 6.6.
[2]John Chrysostom, *Homilies on St. John*, III.6.

better way to promote such feminist teaching than to have a woman standing at the altar?

A wise man like C. S. Lewis realized this obvious connection some years ago. He readily saw that the ordination of women and the reversal of biblical language -- calling God, "Mother," Christ, "daughter," and the Bridegroom, "the Bride" -- were inextricably related. "All this," he wrote, "is involved in the claim that a woman can represent God as a priest does." For this reason, Lewis believed that the ordination of women was most injurious to the Christian Faith: "A child who has been taught to pray to a Mother in Heaven would have a religious life radically different from that of a Christian child."[1] Likewise, the distinguished Orthodox theologian, the Rt. Revd. Dr. Alexander Schmemann, states that the ordination of women would be "tantamount for us to a radical and irreparable mutilation of the entire faith, the rejection of the whole Scripture. . . ."[2] Dr. William Oddie warns that to ordain women as priests is "to change at its foundations our idea of God."[3]

The issue of women's ordination is related not only to feminist theology, the cause of inclusive language for God, the Doctrine of the Incarnation, and our basic Christian understanding of the Trinity, but to Christian morality and all the other sexual liberation issues with which the Church is now wrestling, including the blessing of same sex unions and the ordination of practicing homosexuals. It is important that we see how all these things connect.

C. S. Lewis employs the word "innovators" to describe those advocating the ordination of women; his term applies equally well to those pushing all these other items in the "new" sexual agenda. Lewis says that the "innovators are really implying that

[1]C. S. Lewis, "Priestesses in the Church?," p. 237.
[2]Alexander Schmemann, "Concerning Women's Ordination, in *Sexuality - Theology - Priesthood*, ed. H. K. Lutge, p. 12. This article also appeared in *St. Vladimir's Theology Quarterly*, XVII, 3 (1973).
[3]William Oddie, *What Will Happen to God?*, p. 26.

sex is something superficial, irrelevant to the spiritual life" and treating both men and women "as neuters."[1] If sex is irrelevant, then God's revelation of Himself as Father doesn't matter, nor God's creation of humankind as male and female, nor Christ's Incarnation as a male, nor His choosing male Apostles, nor His teachings about Christian marriage and sexual morality.

All these issues, sooner or later, come down to a choice between the clear witness of Scripture and contemporary opinions, between divine revelation and human experience, between God's order and a new Gnosticism. To reject Holy Scripture for a thoroughly secular agenda, for the latest social and political causes, is to embrace an exceedingly worldly and watered-down "Christianity." Dr. Robert Crouse characterizes this reduction of the Faith to human opinions and theories as "ecclesiastical apostasy, a kind of willful, self-secularizing of the Church." Such an impoverished version of Christianity, says Canon Crouse, "hears no news from heaven and seeks no home beyond this world."[2] Yet true liberation is found only in heaven: "But Jerusalem which is above is free, which is the mother of us all" (*Gal.* 4:26).

Majority Opinion and Votes

One of the most frequently heard arguments in support of the ordination of women is that the majority of people, both in and outside the Church, favour it. One hears similar arguments about cohabitation, abortion, euthanasia, or capital punishment. In the fourth century, the majority of the Church was decidedly under the control of Arianism; its heretical teachings were even upheld by a series of synods.[3] One recalls the famous remark of St. Jerome: "The whole world groaned and marvelled to find itself Arian."[4]

[1]C. S. Lewis, "Priestesses in the Church?," p. 237.

[2]R. D. Crouse, "Concluding Remarks," *A Need for a Catholic Voice in the Church Today*, ed. G. R. Bridge (St. Peter Publications, 1981), p.79.

[3]See J. N. D. Kelly, *Early Christian Doctrines*, 2nd ed. (Harper & Row, 1960), p. 238.

[4]Jerome, *Altercatio Luciferiani et orthodoxi* (c. 379), 19.

Just because the majority approves of something, or experiences it, or practices it, certainly does not make it right or in accordance with divine will. Often just the opposite is true. God called Israel, a tiny and insignificant nation, to be His chosen people. The Christian church began with a minority of One on the cross and a minority of only Twelve in the Upper Room. Minorities are often the way to go!

The Christian Faith is not formulated on the basis of popular ballot, of everyone voting for it. Christianity is a revealed religion, with its basic content given by God. The Church is fundamentally a theocracy, not a democracy, not a majority rule. Her truth does not depend on whether the majority favour it or not. In fact the majority rarely embrace truth. As the spiritual authority, Hans Urs von Balthasar, writes, "It is laughable to take a vote about truths of faith. In a Church which is essentially the 'little flock,' it is not the majority which is right; it never has been and today it is so less than ever."[1]

The majority of church-goers, for example, may have difficulty with the Doctrines of the Virgin Birth or the Resurrection, but this ought not to make us drop these biblical teachings from the ancient creeds. Although, in the hierarchy of truth, the ordination of women cannot be seen at the same level of importance as these credal affirmations, it nevertheless is well grounded in Scripture and Tradition, and for many of us represents God's will for His Church. Therefore, as indicated earlier, it is not a matter of mutable canon law and does not fall in the purview of synods. It is not like changing dates on the church calendar, amending disciplinary canons, or adjusting clergy pension plans, but is a tampering with divine revelation and order. It involves much more than discipline, more than what Hooker calls "matters of regiment,"[2] but touches upon the Doctrines of the Creation, Incarnation, Redemption, and Trinity, the validity of Sacraments, and the essential unity of the Church.

[1]H. U. von Balthasar, *Elucidations*, trans. John Riches (SPCK, 1975), p. 95. Jesus, of course, calls His disciples His "little flock" (*Lk.*12:32).
[2]Richard Hooker, *Of the Laws of Ecclesiastical Polity*, III.10.7.

Were synods competent to vote on the matter of women priests -- and I don't believe that they are! -- there would still be questions about proceeding on the basis of simple majorities. At the 1976 General Convention of the American Episcopal Church (ECUSA), the ordination of women passed by six votes or a margin of less than one per cent. At the November, 1992, General Synod of the Church of England, the ordination of women legislation obtained the required two-thirds majority among the laity by a narrow margin of two votes.

Narrow majorities is not how the Apostolic Church dealt with controversial matters, such as opening up the church to Gentiles and abolishing the rite of circumcision. The Apostles proceeded not on a majority vote of 51%, 66.66%, or even 75%, but on consensus, the whole body arriving at what it believed was the will of God, the mind of Christ. At Pentecost the Apostles were "with one accord" (*Acts* 2:1); and when controversy arose in the mission field and the first council was called, a decision was reached which pleased "the Apostles and Elders, with the whole Church" (*Acts* 15:22). In the official letters of the Council, the Apostles could say: "It seemeth good unto *us*, being assembled with one accord" (15:25) and "it seemeth good to the Holy Ghost, and to us" (15:28).

In this same conciliar spirit, St. Paul calls upon the Corinthians: "That ye all speak the same thing, and that there be no divisions among you, but that ye be perfectly joined together in the same mind and the same judgement" (*1 Cor.* 1:10). Also, St. Paul urges the Philippians to be "like-minded, having the same love, being of one accord, of one mind" (2:2). These passages are not about being thoughtless or opinionless vegetables but about acting on the basis of consensus, not simple majorities, and thus avoiding schism and confusion in the Body of Christ.

Man-made Laws vs. Divine Edicts

Related to arguments about majority votes is the idea that many parts of the Anglican Church, through their respective synods, have officially and legally adopted the ordination of

113

women, have expressed their political will. Once again, just because something is legal doesn't make it right. Abortion is legally permitted by civil authority, but for many it is morally reprehensible, contrary to divine law. Cohabitation is legal, but it is something less than God's institution of Holy Matrimony. God's order is revealed by Him, not legislated by us.

I have already argued that the Church, her Ministry, and Sacraments are of divine institution; hence, they are governed by a divine constitution. Bishop Jeremy Taylor, for example, insists that the priesthood "must depend upon God's acceptance and therefore upon divine constitution."[1] Bishop Thomas Brett speaks of the Church as a "Body-Politic," which has received her "original charter" from Christ, "the one only Supreme Head of the Church." Dr. Brett writes that the Church's sovereign Lord

did also set and appoint over this Spiritual City, this Heavenly Kingdom, several Officers, Magistrates, or Governors to rule this Society, and to govern this Church under Him according to the Laws which He had prescribed for it. . . .[2]

Christ, not men, constituted the Church and her Apostolic Ministry. Christ, not men, gave the Church her charter and commission; He prescribed her fundamental, incontrovertible laws, including those which govern the Apostolic Ministry "at all times, and in all places." Therefore, any legislation to sanction women priests and bishops is, both spiritually and theologically, unconstitutional, a gross violation of the original charter granted by Christ, who did only what pleased the Father (*Jn.* 8:29).

All the same, it should be noted that the new, man-man canons giving women clergy legal standing in this world were, at least initially, permissive, not mandatory, canons.[3] They stated that women *may* be ordained, not that they must be and not that

[1]Jeremy Taylor, *Of the Office Ministerial*, 6.1.

[2]Thomas Brett, *An Account of Church Government* (1710), I. 8.

[3]An informative history of the permissive interpretation of ECUSA's legislation on women priests will be found in William C. Wantland, *The Catholic Faith, the Episcopal Church, and the Ordination of Women*, pp. 23-37. Bishop Wantland's background as a lawyer, judge, and law professor especially qualify him to write this legal history.

everyone must agree with or accept their ordination. It would be impossible to legislate such consensus, although hard-line proponents of women's ordination are certainly trying to make the practice mandatory, in very legalistic and Pharisaical ways. Synods are using their legal powers to crush any opposition. For example, the 1997 General Convention of the American Episcopal Church, meeting in Philadelphia, amended Canon III.8.1., in a concerted effort to make the ordination of women a legal requirement in every diocese.[1] Unfortunately, reason, tolerance, and goodwill appear to be in ever diminishing supply these days; and, realistically, we can expect more mandatory canons, Pharisaism, and litigation.

If we are faced with choosing between what is legal and what we believe is right, of course, we have a Christian duty to choose what is right. This *modus operandi* has noteworthy Apostolic precedence. St. Peter and the Apostles found themselves bound to answer the high priest: "We ought to obey God rather than men" (*Acts* 5:29).

Infallibility of Synods?
The chief political mechanisms of the contemporary Church, and indeed much of her undoing, are her synods. These political bodies are large, unwieldy, self-consuming, and self-serving. Synods have never been perfect bodies, untainted by the sinful love of power and political intrigue. St. Gregory Nazianzus (329-89), Bishop and Doctor of the Church, who attended the great Council of Constantinople (381), wrote that his inclination was "to avoid all synods." He explains:

---

[1]It is noteworthy that as recently as 1989, the American Bishops declared that "there is not a common theological mind or agreed practice" on women priests and that "those who believe that women should not be ordained hold a recognized theological position" (Wantland, *Op cit.*, p. 30). It is even more remarkable that as recently as 1994, ECUSA's Committee for Dialogue on Canon III.8.1. stated: "General Convention acknowledges that those who support and those who oppose the ordination of women to the priesthood and episcopate each hold a recognized theological position in this Church" (p. 32). In a space of only three years, that tolerance has all but evaporated.

I have never seen any synod come to a good end nor turn out to be a solution of evils. On the contrary, it usually increases them. You always find there love of contention and love of power, which beggar description."[1]

Contrary to St. Gregory's estimation of synodical shortcomings, many Anglicans have enormous, unrealistic confidence in their synods. Delegates get caught up in the synodical system and its worldly politics, forgetting that the Church is a divine institution with a message and mission from God. Years ago Bishop John Wordsworth (1843-1911) wrote of "the danger of being in love with system: of treating it as an end in itself and of confusing the Church with the conditions of the life of the Church on earth."[2] This confusion allows synodical bodies to take on an authority and infallibility which they do not have, and they begin to suffer from the delusion that they can somehow overturn the teaching of Scripture and the Tradition of the Universal Church. Synods are collectively guilty of that pride which St. Paul delineates; thinking of themselves "more highly than they ought to think" (*Rom.* 12:3).

To guard against this kind of synodical pride and arrogance, is why, according to Archbishop Philip Carrington (1892-1975), autonomous Anglican Churches have adopted solemn declarations or fundamental statements about those things which cannot be changed and which strictly limit the authority of synods. Archbishop Carrington explains that these declarations

> require fidelity to the Prayer Book and other formularies as permanent standards of doctrine and worship; and of course to the ancient creeds and to the sacramental order and to the Apostolic Ministry which we have received through the Church of England from the primitive undivided Church, and hold in common with the whole Anglican Communion throughout the world, and indeed with all the older churches of the Catholic tradition.[3]

[1]Gregory Nazianzus, in a letter to Procopius, the Prefect of Constantinople. Cited in W. R. Inge, *The Fall of the Idols* (Putnam, 1940), pp. 297-98.

[2]John Wordsworth, *The Ministry of Grace* (Longmans, 1908), p. 143.

[3]Philip Carrington, *The Anglican Church in Canada* (Collins, 1963), p. 131.

116

Similarly, the Committee on the Anglican Communion, which Archbishop Carrington chaired at the 1948 Lambeth Conference, reported that a dispersed authority, "distributed among Scripture, Tradition, Creeds, the Ministry of the Word and Sacraments, the witness of saints, and the *consensus fidelium*" is a strength and blessing to Anglicans; it is "God's loving provision against the temptations to tyranny and the dangers of unchecked power."[1]

Finally, it must be pointed out that no bishop, priest, or deacon, at his ordination, takes any vow to uphold Anglican synods. Ordinands do, however, promise to uphold the teachings of Scripture[2] and to "drive away all erroneous and strange doctrines" contrary to the same.[3]

Infallibility of Bishops?

Priests and deacons also promise at their ordinations to obey their bishops,[4] but this is not blind, unqualified, absolute obedience. One promises to follow the bishop's *"godly* admonitions" and submit to his *"godly* judgements." Likewise, the traditional Oaths of Obedience in the Anglican Church are made to the Bishop and his successors "in all things lawful and honest."[5] It is obvious that a matter such as the ordination of women, which many of us believe to be the overthrow of divine order, cannot be considered *godly.* Neither can episcopal pronouncements about this be *godly.* When confronted with a choice between scriptural truth and a bishop's or synod's opinions, there should be no difficulty. "It is everyone's duty," Pusey told Keble, "to maintain catholic truth, even if unhappily opposed by a Bishop."[6]

No matter what foolish things synods say or authorize, it

---

[1] *The Lambeth Conference 1948* (SPCK, 1948), pp. 84-85.

[2] *Book of Common Prayer*, pp. 641, 651, 663.

[3] *Ibid.*, pp. 652 & 663.

[4] *Ibid.*, pp. 642 & 653.

[5] English Canon Law, C-14.

[6] E. B. Pusey (1842), cited in Standish Meacham, *Lord Bishop: the Life of Samuel Wilberforce, 1805-1873* (Harvard University Press, 1970), p. 174.

takes the hands of a bishop to attempt to ordain a woman, to make the actual break with the Apostles. Bishops, who by their office are called to be guardians of Apostolic faith and practice and the sign and focus of unity in the Church, cannot be excused from their major role in our present crisis. Disappointment in bishops is nothing new. As John Henry Newman points out, in his book on the Arian heresy: "The Catholic people, in the length and breadth of Christendom, were the obstinate champions of Catholic truth, and the bishops were not."[1]

The historical record alone should save us from any romantic notions of bishops or blind trust in them. Such a realistic stance is often interpreted as being congregationalist, anti-diocese, or anti-bishop. This is not true in that Traditionalists have the highest regard for the office of bishop and are those most apt to defend episcopal office as part of divine order. But we must never confuse the office of bishop with an individual occupying a particular see or with his private, small, and erroneous ideas.

We have a duty to pray for our bishops, who, like us all, are sinners under judgment. We must pray that our bishops will stand against the political pressures of the day, be true guardians of the faith, and be faithful to their ordination promises to live under the authority of Scripture. In his treatise on bishops, Jeremy Taylor says that "Christ did institute a government to order and rule his Church by his authority, according to his laws, and by the assistance of the blessed Spirit."[2] Bishops are not exempt from Christ's authority and His laws.

We must also pray that our bishops will be true pastors to the flock and fellow servants in Christ, not wolves in sheep's clothing, not prelatical autocrats, or tyrants. In speaking about his and other bishops' spiritual role as guardian, shepherd, and master, St. Augustine says "we ourselves desire to be guarded together with you. . .under that Shepherd we are fellow-sheep

[1] J. H. Newman, *The Arians of the Fourth Century*, 3rd ed. (London, 1871), p. 454. See G. Leonard, *Firmly I Believe and Truly* (Mowbray, 1985), p. 6.
[2] Jeremy Taylor, *Of the Sacred Order and Offices of Episcopacy*, 1.

together with you. . . under that One Master, we are school-fellows with you . . . ."[1] May our bishops once again realize that they are our fellow-disciples, under "that One Master."

Politicalization of the Spirit

Those who seem to control synods and bishops and who have "won" the political and legal battles of the day, including the ordination of women, often claim that they are being ruled by the Holy Spirit. Oddly enough, these same people never accepted the negative votes at previous synods as the voice of the Holy Spirit! Many are very sincere in believing that their recent victories are inspired by the Spirit, and I certainly do not question their sincerity. However, I am wary of the glibness with which we can say that the Holy Spirit has sanctioned this or that, making Him a rubber stamp for decisions we have taken, individually or collectively. We seem to blame lots on the Holy Spirit. We have an affinity with the cartoon character, Dennis the Menace, who used to blame everything on the Devil and who wore a T-shirt which read: "The Devil made me do it."

Furthermore, I am equally convinced that the Holy Spirit has told me and others that the ordination of women is wrong. Our understanding of the Spirit's direction could be just as subjective and full of error. But there is in our position, I believe, an objectivity which is vitally important, and which supporters of women priests seem to lack. Life in the Spirit is not wholly subjective or emotional; it insists upon an objectivity which saves us from "feel-good," "do-your-own-thing" religion.

The Spirit, objectively and clearly, speaks to us through the teachings of Holy Scripture; the Spirit calls to mind what our Lord taught and what He did (*Jn.* 14.26 and 16:13-14).   The Spirit speaks to us through the Apostles, what they taught and what they did,   and a consistent Tradition of 2,000 years. Archbishop Michael Ramsey (1904-88) reminds us that life in the

---

[1]Augustine, *Enarrationes in Psalmos,* 126 (Prayerbook #127). In a sermon at the consecration of a bishop (Carthage, 412), St. Augustine observed: "we are servants; we are at your head, but only if we are at your side."

Holy Spirit is not only "a life of new adventures and discoveries" but also "a life of continuing witness to the history whereby it has been created." Ramsey speaks about "certain media of continuity through which the Spirit acts in the Church's common life," specifically mentioning "the Sacraments, the Apostolic Ministry, and a tradition of teaching."[1]

It should be noted that as recently as 1935, the Archbishops' Commission on the Ministry of Women concluded that "the continuous tradition" of a male priesthood was of the Holy Spirit: "It is our conviction that this consensus of tradition and opinion is based upon the will of God and is, for the Church of today, a sufficient witness to the guidance of the Holy Spirit."[2] Sixty-five years ago is not very long in a 2,000 year Tradition! What would make the Holy Spirit change His mind in the last fifty or sixty years?

Individual women often say that they feel called to the ordained ministry by the Holy Spirit. There can be no question that the Spirit is calling them to ministry, but is it to Apostolic orders? Would not the Spirit make such a call obvious to His whole church? Would the Spirit, after speaking consistently through Scripture and 2,000 years of Holy Tradition, make a dramatic about face? Would the Spirit, "the Lord and Giver of Life," contradict himself? Would the Holy Spirit withhold something essential and necessary from the Church for nearly 2,000 years? What would this say about divine guidance or the Providence of God? What would this say about the relationship of the Spirit to the Father and the Son? Is the Spirit not co-essential, co-eternal, and co-equal with the Father and the Son?

Finally, let us not forget what Scripture lists as the fruit of the Spirit: "love, joy, peace, longsuffering, gentleness, goodness,

[1] A. M. Ramsey, *The Holy Spirit* (London, 1977), p. 86.
[2] *The Ministry of Women* (Church House, Westminster, 1935), p. 9. This conclusion is repeated, almost verbatim, on p. 29 of the Report. The Report was fully endorsed by twelve members of the Commission, with a minority report submitted by its thirteenth member.

faith, meekness, temperance" (*Gal.* 5:22-23). Such fruit is not very evident in our extremely polarized, disordered Church, where, to quote Yeats, "Things fall apart; the centre cannot hold."[1] St. Paul writes elsewhere, actually just before his injunction about women keeping silence: "God is not the author of confusion, but of peace" (*1 Cor.* 14:33). Could an issue as divisive and disruptive as the ordination of women truly be of the Spirit? Does it manifest the peace and gentleness, the harmony and unanimity, of the Spirit? Does it edify the whole Body?

The Spirit of the Age

What is often attributed to the voice of the Holy Spirit could just as easily be the spirit of the age, the *Zeitgeist.* Secular pressures and influences can make us feel many things and feel them powerfully. Many of us have strong ideas about social justice and human rights issues, and these vigorous personal opinions and feelings can stir us up and move us to political and social action. However, we must not confuse these ideological promptings, "the devices and desires of our own hearts,"[2] with the perfect and eternal will of God and with the inspiration of the Holy Spirit (*der heilige Geist,* not any other *Geist!*).

As the Church, we are called to be faithful to God's will, not to worldly pressure tactics or modern notions of relevancy. How can anyone really love or respect a Church which is inseparable from the pagan culture? Jesus plainly taught that his kingdom "is not of this world" (*Jn.* 18:36), that the world would hate His followers as it hated Him (*Jn.* 15:18-19), and that they should "lay up treasures in heaven" (*Mt.* 6:20). St. Paul tells the Romans not to be "conformed to this world" (*Rom.* 12:2), and he reminds the Philippians that "our citizenship is in heaven" (*Phil.* 3:20). *Hebrews* reminds us that "here have we no continuing city" (*Heb. 13:14),* and St. John instructs the Faithful: "Love not the world, neither the things that are in the world" (*1 Jn.* 2:15). From *the Acts of the Apostles* and several of the New Testament epistles, we learn that the Apostles frequently found themselves

[1] William Butler Yeats, "The Second Coming," line 3.
[2] A General Confession, *Book of Common Prayer,* p. 5.

in fierce opposition to the world, a world which misunder-
stood and despised them and even martyred them. Surely this
same world must not be allowed to set the Church's agenda.

The Church, on the other hand, must help the world to
conform to her agenda, God's unchanging agenda. As "the salt
of the earth" and "the light of the world" (*Mt.* 5:13-14), we are
not to mirror this transitory realm but to show an unsavoury and
dark world the way to a glorious kingdom beyond here and now,
to something that outlives present-day politics and sociology,
something beyond feminism and other "isms," something far
more important than the *Zeitgeist*. Dr. William Ralph Inge (1860-
1954), one of the great Deans of St. Paul's Cathedral, London,
wisely counsels that we immortal spirits "should not degrade
ourselves by worrying too much about the *Zeitgeist*." He
admonishes: "Do not sacrifice your own soul to the fads of this
generation. They are not worth it."[1] In a similar vein, C. S.
Lewis remarks: "All that is not eternal is eternally out of date."[2]

God did not become man so that He could repeat our
mistakes. He was not incarnate in order to adapt Himself more
closely to our worldly standards, to live by our latest social and
political insights, to be "politically correct." He came to save us
from the hell of ourselves, to show us the way beyond ourselves
-- in each and every way, to bring us back to the Father.

Dr. Philip Edgcumbe Hughes (1915-90) argued that in the
specific case of the ordination of women, our choice is clearly
between God's order and "secular fashions and pressures of our
day . . . between God's cosmos and man's chaos."[3]   Similarly,
Dr. Peter Toon says that the Church's

[1]W. R. Inge, *The Church and the Age* (Longmans, Green, 1912), p. 42. In
these addresses, Dean Inge distinguishes between "the Spirit (or Spirits) of the
Age" and "the Spirit of the Ages" (that is, the Holy Spirit).   Dr. Inge's oft-
quoted aphorism is most pertinent: "Whoever marries the spirit of this age will
find himself a widower in the next."
[2]C. S. Lewis, *The Four Loves* (Collins, 1977), p. 125.
[3]Philip Edgcumbe Hughes, *The Evangelical Catholic,* 1 March, 1979.

ordained ministry does not exist to symbolize and express what the modern world regards as vitally important but rather to be and do what the Lord Jesus desires. His word tells us that he wants male presbyters and bishops.[1]

In this matter, as in all others, should we not discern and obey Christ's will for His Church?

More representative?

Proponents of women's ordination often argue that an all-male priesthood is not only unjust but somehow incomplete and not fully representative. We must ask: Representative of whom or what?

A convincing argument could be made if the priesthood is simply about representing the whole human race before God, that is, representing the two sexes, Adam and Eve, man and woman. Of course, a rebuttal could be offered based on the creation narrative: Since woman was made from man, man can represent both sexes in a way that woman cannot. On the other hand, one could argue that from Adam and Eve onwards man is born of woman; both sexes are necessary for procreation and the continuance of humankind, and both should be included in, and representative of, the Church's ministry.

Should one push this representational thesis too far, then neither a man nor a woman could ever be seen as fully human or ever capable of representing humanity. Neither a male nor a female priest could by himself or herself ever represent the whole Church, the redeemed community. At each and every Eucharist one would have to arrange for co-celebrants, at least one male priest and one female priest! After a while, this could become quite silly.

If proponents of women's ordination seriously and literally mean that a male priest cannot truly represent humanity, there are far-reaching, theological implications. For this line of argument would raise alarming questions about Christ's own

[1]Peter Toon, *Let Women Be Women*, p. 115.

123

High Priesthood, about His Incarnation and saving work among us, about His heavenly intercession for us, and, therefore, about God's wisdom, omniscience, and providence.

The insistence on a more representative priesthood -- that is, a joint male and female priesthood -- logically implies that our High Priest, incarnate as a male, was, and is, unable to represent our entire humanity. It would suggest that His Incarnation as a male was a terrible mistake and that He was somehow a failure, an imperfect, deficient person and not a fully representative Saviour and Risen Lord. It would insinuate that His dying on the cross was not for the sins of the whole world, not for both men and women, not for all of humanity. It would intimate that in His Ascension, our Lord did not take our full humanity, but only the male sex, into the Godhead. It would mean, in the words of Dr. Graham Leonard, that "our redemption is incomplete and that the Gospel which the Church has been proclaiming for two thousand years is inadequate."[1]

Such reasoning would eventually lead one to conclude that Christ, in order to be a truly representative and effective Redeemer and High Priest, should have been born as both man and woman, as a hermaphrodite, or that there should have been a second incarnation as a woman.

God obviously was not convinced by such arguments because, once and for all time, He sent His only begotten Son to die for all of us, both men and women. What He actually did is far more important than what we wish that He had done.

Further representation?
In addition, it must be emphasized that the priest's calling is to represent more than humankind, more than men and women, more than the Church, more than "the people of God." Archbishop Michael Ramsey, who calls the priest "the man of the Eucharist," writes:

[1]Graham Leonard, "The Priesthood of Christ," in *Man, Woman, & Priesthood,* ed. J. Tolhurst, p. 20.

As celebrant he is more than the people's representative. In taking, breaking, and consecrating, he acts in Christ's name and in the name not only of the particular congregation but of the Holy Catholic Church down the ages.[1]

As explained in my third chapter, a significant, symbolic role of the priest -- liturgically, sacramentally, and theologically -- is to represent God the Father and Jesus Christ His only-begotten Son. This is very evident in traditional liturgical settings where the priest turns from the altar to pronounce God's absolution and blessing. C. S. Lewis makes much of this in his thoughtful essay about women priests. Lewis, as both a literary scholar and a theologian, understood the importance of proper images: "Sometimes the priest turns his back on us and faces the East -- he speaks to God for us: sometimes he faces us and speaks to us for God."[2] Regardless of liturgical orientation, the celebrant stands in the place of Christ, who was incarnate as a male, and who is the perfect revelation of God the Father. The priest, as an icon of Christ, says "This is my body" and "This is my blood" and consecrates the elements. The priest acts *in persona Christi* ("in the person of Christ"), not simply *in persona ecclesiae* ("in the person of the Church").

This same sacramental principle also applies, of course, to bishops. Archbishop William Temple explains it well:

When I consecrate a godly and well-learned man to the office and rank of a bishop in the Church of God, I do not act as a representative of the Church, if by that is meant the whole number of contemporary Christians; but I do act as the ministerial instrument of Christ in His Body the Church. The authority by which I act is His, transmitted to me through his Apostles and those to whom they committed it; I hold it neither from the Church nor apart from the Church, but from Christ in the Church.[3]

[1]A. M. Ramsey, *The Christian Priest Today* (SPCK, 1972), pp. 9-10.
[2]C. S. Lewis, "Priestesses in the Church?," p. 236.
[3]William Temple, "*Christian Unity and Church Reunion* (1943), pp. 18-19. Cited by K. E. Kirk in his introductory article in *The Apostolic Ministry*, pp. 32-33.

Bishops, like priests, represent more than the human family, more than the Church.

Finally, it must again be said that our great High Priest, Jesus Christ, the only-begotten Son of God, appointed male Apostles and their successors to represent Him. He did not see the need for a female priesthood, a two-sex priesthood, nor an hermaphroditic priesthood. A male priesthood was clearly His choice. It was, and is, representative for Him, and it ought to be for us too.

Experience

When more serious theological arguments fail, proponents of women's ordination sometimes resort to experiential evidence. For example, we often hear bishops saying how positive the experience of women priests has been. Even people who were once opposed, they argue, have come to accept the Sacraments from women priests. Undoubtedly, many people have changed their position. Some claim to have been "converted," and there is no reason to doubt them.

All experience, however, is not so rosy. What about all the people who have spoken with their feet and who have left the Anglican Church? What about all those who stay but who have not been convinced by the experience? What about the many good people who simply don't like making ripples, let alone waves? What about the many who dissent privately and silently? What about those who are simply weary of battle? What about all the consciences that have been violated? What about all the hurt that has been caused? What about all the distrust? Could we not be very selective in the kind of experience we recognize and report?

But experience alone, be it happy or sad, on one side or the other, does not really justify anything. Experience can simply get us accustomed to improper ideas or practices, move us to accept false norms, and teach us to embrace things which may not be good or right for us. One can have a very happy and enjoyable

126

experience eating high caloric and fatty foods, or smoking cigarettes, or drinking a bottle of vodka. But the experience alone does not justify or vindicate the vice, does not make it any healthier or better for us. There must be a more objective basis upon which we can examine serious theological matters, such as the testimony of Scripture and Tradition.

The Sacraments, including Holy Orders, do not depend upon our experience of them, but they have a more realistic and objective basis, a deeper grounding, a firmer foundation. Austin Farrer explained this in wonderfully graphic terms:

Apples don't drop from the sky; they grow on apple trees. And sacraments don't hurtle down here and there like lightning from heaven: they grow on the great branching tree of the Apostles' ministry, the tree planted by Christ when he called twelve men and made them his ambassadors; a tree which has grown and spread and thrown its arms out all through history, to fill the whole earth.[1]

That is a truly Catholic perspective, an historical and objective view, a sacramental understanding.

Therefore, if we cannot stop talking about *experience*, at least let us talk about a broader, wiser, and more authoritative experience. At the 1968 Lambeth Conference, Archbishop Athenagoras II, said: "When we depart from the Apostolic *experience*, we do not contribute to the unity of Christianity."[2] The Greek archbishop has something to teach us: let us begin to talk about the Apostles' *experience* more than our own. That could be a way of staying in touch with Catholic norms, safeguarding Catholic Sacraments, and also preserving the unity of the Church.

Misogynists

Some advocates of women priests resort to *ad hominem* attacks, insinuating that proponents of an all-male ministry,

[1]Austin Farrer, "Walking Sacraments," *A Celebration of Faith*, p. 109.

[2]Athenagoras, cited in J. B. Simpson & E. M. Story, *The Long Shadows of Lambeth X*, p. 162.

especially men, have a dislike of women or are even hardened misogynists. This, of course, is preposterous. Many of us who affirm the male priesthood, both men and women, have the most genuine love and highest respect for women: for our mothers, grandmothers, and sisters, for wives, and daughters and nieces, and female friends. Many of us are what we are because of dedicated women teachers and professors, who inspired us along the way. Many of us have every confidence in women professionals, entrusting our health care to women physicians, dentists, and other health workers, entrusting our legal and business affairs to women lawyers and executives. Many of us are loyal subjects of Her Majesty the Queen. Many of us have worked closely with women wardens, chaplains, nuns, and other female church leaders. Many of us have great religious devotion to the Blessed Virgin Mary and to other women saints.

Opposition to women priests does not translate opposition to women. A superb example is the present Pope, John Paul II, who in one Apostolic Letter, *Ordinatio Sacerdotalis,* has made a definitive statement that priests must be male. However, in another Apostolic Letter, *Mulieris Dignitatem*, His Holiness has written a very positive and celebrative work about Christian women, upholding their dignity and unique roles.[1] The two Apostolic Letters are not in the least contradictory.

A case could be made that those who strongly believe that women should perform men's functions in the Church are, in fact, the ones demeaning women, suggesting that women have no gifts and charismata of their own. This was true of the Gnostics, who believed that sexual differentiation was totally unimportant and who, therefore, accepted women priests. There is, of course, a certain irony and illogic in modern feminist theology assimilating Gnostic tendencies. For Gnosticism does not value the feminine, nor for that matter the masculine, but holds up the androgynous as the ideal. One of the conclusions in Manfred Hauke's magisterial study is that a demand for female priesthood

[1]John Paul II, *Mulieris Dignitatem* ("On the Dignity and Vocation of Women"), 1988.

"ultimately stems -- whether consciously or unconsciously -- from a gnostic-like contempt for women."[1]

Who is divisive?

A favourite political strategy of the "liberal" majority in the Church is to accuse the Traditionalist minority of being dissidents, causing unhappy division, being disloyal, even operating illegally. In fairness, all the Traditionalists ask is that they be allowed to remain faithful to that which they have been taught.

Any division has in fact been caused by those who have intentionally altered the Church's received Tradition and overturned God-given sacramental order. St. Cyprian grasped this well:

> But what unity is maintained, what love practised or even imagined by one who, mad with the frenzy of discord, splits the Church, destroys the faith, disturbs the peace, casts charity to the winds, desecrates the Sacrament?[2]

Dr. Pusey also explains this principle elegantly in a letter to the Archbishop of Canterbury concerning a possible schism over the attempts to revise the Athanasian Creed or remove it from the Prayer-book. He assures Dr. Tait that the division would not be of the Traditionalists' making but would entirely be the responsibility of the revisionists:

> The rent would be caused, not by us -- who should be cast out of our homes, who would have to sacrifice all the cherished hopes of our lives -- but by those (whoever they may be) who would trample upon our consciences, and the consciences of the laity who are faithful to the old belief.[3]

The Encyclical of the First Lambeth Conference (1867) echoes Pusey's words when it counsels: "Hold fast the Creeds and the pure worship and order, which of God's grace ye have inherited from the Primitive Church. Beware of causing divisions contrary

[1]Manfred Hauke, *Women in the Priesthood?*, p. 471.

[2]Cyprian, *De ecclesiae catholicae unitate*, 15.

[3]E. B. Pusey, Letter of 12 October, 1872, in H. P. Liddon, *Life of Edward Bouverie Pusey*, IV (1897), 250-51.

to the doctrine ye have received."[1]   Note carefully who, according to the first Lambeth Fathers, are the cause of division: those who turn their backs on the doctrine received from the Apostles, those who abandon the Faith once delivered, those who chop down Dr. Farrer's apple tree, "the great branching tree of the Apostles' ministry."

A dying breed?

Another political tactic of the "liberal" majority is to suggest that those opposed to women priests are a dying breed. If this were true and all opposition to female priests is dying a natural death, then why do so many bishops and other proponents of women's ordination always seem to be on the defensive? Why do they incessantly talk about this subject, heavy-handedly push it at every opportunity, constantly harp on its canonical and legal standing, and labour to give it more and more legal protection?

It would appear that many proponents of women's ordination are, consciously or unconsciously, deeply threatened and insecure in their position. It would suggest that there is something remarkably fragile about the cause of women priests and bishops. Maybe there is a terrible fear that opposition will not retreat to the woods like a dying animal and quietly wait to die.

As one engaged in university chaplaincy for twenty years, I must point out that any suggestion that opposition to women priests is slowly dying is blatantly untrue. To paraphrase Mark Twain (1835-1910),   "The report of our death is an exaggeration."[2]   Many young people, both men and women, are Traditionalists. In some ways a number of them are far more Traditionalist than I am! (That allegation really should strike fear in the hearts of liberals!) These thoughtful young people look to traditional values in a way that the Church's present leadership, largely trained in the radical 1960s, can not.

[1]*The Six Lambeth Conferences, 1867-1920* (SPCK, 1920), p. 51
[2]When American newspapers mistakenly reported his death, Mark Twain sent a cable from Europe to the Associated Press: "The report of my death was an exaggeration."

God continues to call many young Traditionalist men to His Apostolic Ministry. This is also true in the Church of Sweden, which has had women priests since 1961, considerably longer than any Anglican Church. Yet the "resistance" movement continues to be strong in Sweden, and Traditionalists in that church have formed a vigorous Free Synod movement.

We must accept the political and spiritual reality of the present-day church: Traditionalists are not going to curl up and die. If illiberal liberals have their way, Traditionalists may well be forced out of certain national churches; but they will simply regroup and resurface, in the meanwhile made stronger and more determined by their days of persecution. They will not disappear, and to think otherwise is indeed wishful and totally unrealistic. God continues to call and to raise up people who are faithful to Scripture and the Apostolic Tradition.

No turning back?
Some hold such a fatalistic view of the world and society that they believe that there is no turning around, no going back, not ever. Now that women have been ordained bishops and priests, they are here to stay, like it or lump it. *Fait accompli!*

Such a view cannot be defended historically. Second-century heresies ordained women, and with the ascent of orthodoxy, the practice died a natural death. The Polish Mariavite Church, which ordained women for some fifty years, decided twenty-five years ago to stop. In 1991, the Presbyterian Church in Australia voted to reverse its 1974 decision to ordain women. I know a number of individual Anglicans who were initially in favour of women priests and who have now changed their minds. Over a long period of time, this trend could accelerate. Church history clearly shows us that minorities have a way of becoming majorities, and there is no reason to think that the Anglican Church is exempt from such historical realities.

I believe that in due course -- not in my lifetime, but in due course -- the Anglican Church may well reverse its un-Catholic and un-Apostolic decision to ordain women. It will require a considerable degree of humility, but I do believe that the Church will submit to God's will and mend her ways. However, such a long-term view in no way precludes Traditionalists from having to establish new provinces and structures within Anglicanism or having to move elsewhere in the interim. For I believe that before there is a reversal of this decision, there will be increased intolerance, pain, schism, and crumbling of the foundations.

I would be delighted, of course, if I were wrong and the reversal were to come sooner than later. However dim or remote that may seem, we cannot entirely rule it out. The 1988 Lambeth Conference did not rule it out. The Conference said that until reception occurs throughout the Church, matters should never be considered settled and decisions final:

> It is still possible for those decisions to be modified, or even reversed, even though they have been accepted and even acted on by provincial synods and endorsed by a majority of bishops at the Lambeth Conference.[1]

This most refreshing point of view is, after all, only realistic and reasonable. C. S. Lewis asks: "Would you think I was joking if I said that you can put a clock back, and that if the clock is wrong it is often a very sensible thing to do?"[2]

---

[1] "Dogmatic and Pastoral Concerns," in *The Truth Shall Make You Free: The Lambeth Conference 1988*, p. 117.

[2] C. S. Lewis, *Mere Christianity*, p. 22.

Epilogue

Women's Ministry

I firmly believe that according to God's order, revealed in Scripture and maintained throughout Holy Tradition, only men can be ordained Apostolic Ministers. At the same time I firmly believe that women have much to offer to the total ministry of Christ's Church. Unquestionably, women have the full baptismal dignity of Christ; they are complete and *bona fide* members of His Church and belong to the royal priesthood of all believers. Undeniably, women played prominent roles not only in the New Testament Church but in the Church throughout the course of Christian history. As any parish priest can testify, women continue to play extremely important roles in the life of our parishes and dioceses, greatly enriching the Body of Christ.

Ordination is certainly not a prerequisite for service in the Church, neither for women nor for men. Both Christian women and Christian men can be affirmed and encouraged by the Church without being ordained. Certainly women should not feel that they must prove that they can do equally well all the things men do; they must not think that they have to imitate or replicate men. That would be an overtly sexist programme.

Many avenues of service in God's Church are available to women, quite apart from the male ordained ministry. Yet we must be open to new avenues of ministry for women. We have not begun to realize the potential of women's lay ministry in areas such as chaplaincy, hospital visiting, counselling, and administration. Undoubtedly, women have many special gifts and charismata which they can bring to these and other lay ministries in the Church.

Evelyn Underhill, in a splendid essay on women's ministry, says that she has known lay women "who have genuinely ministered to souls in a creative way." She continues:

> The question of status, scope, and so forth has never, I should think, entered their minds at all. Their hidden life of love and prayer. . . has largely exceeded and entirely supported their life of active work.

Later, she writes of these women:

> We notice a sort of beautiful informality and freedom in their proceedings; and something which we might call a maternal and domestic quality in their method, which seems on the whole to look more towards the prophetic than the priestly way of serving God and tending souls.

She refers to these women as "individuals surrendered to the Spirit, moving and working under his pressure, and yet with great freedom and originality, within the institutional frame. . . ."[1]

Our Lady's Example

In affirming the importance of women's ministry in the Church, we must never forget the supreme example of the Blessed Virgin Mary, a lay person upon whom God bestowed a dignity higher than that given to any other human being. For she was chosen by our heavenly Father to be the Mother of God, and the Council of Ephesus gave her the exalted title of *Theotokos* (God-bearer). She is, in the words of Pope John Paul II, "the most complete expression" of the "dignity and vocation" of every Christian.[2] She is worthy of lofty praise, including this rapturous, Anglican verse by Thomas Traherne (1637-74):

> O Lord, I praise and magnify thy Name
> For the Most Holy Virgin-Mother of God,
> Who is the Highest of Thy Saints,
> The most Glorious of all Thy Creatures,
> The Most Perfect of all Thy Works,
> The nearest unto Thee, in the Throne of God.[3]

[1]Evelyn Underhill, "The Ideals of the Ministry of Women," *Mixed Pasture,* pp. 116-118.

[2]John Paul II, *Mulieris Dignitatem*, pp. 20-21.

[3]Thomas Traherne, "A Thanksgiving for the Exhaltation and for the Virtues of the Blessed Virgin," from an unpublished manuscript in the Bodleian Library,

The Blessed Mother is, in the familiar and ecstatic words of one of our finest hymns, "the bearer of the eternal word," and, therefore, "higher than the Cherubim, more glorious than the Seraphim."[1] St. Mary, who is higher than the angels, higher than the Apostles or any saint, is surely higher than any priest or bishop! Ordination could not have bestowed upon her any greater dignity.

In her faith, humility, and devotion, St. Mary is a type or image of the whole Church. The Church, like our Lady, must be the faithful bearer of the Word, the Ark and Temple in which God dwells, the fruitful and life-giving mother who nourishes and cares for her children. The Church, like St. Mary, must also be submissive to her Lord, open and receptive to God's grace. Dr. Peter Toon summarizes this well when he says that "the Church as a whole is Marian, truly feminine, open and ready to receive the energising life and dynamic truth of her Life-giver and Head. . . ."[2]

For all Christians, both men and women, St. Mary is the supreme image and example of the Church at prayer and meditation, the Church waiting upon her Lord, pondering mysteries in her heart. We need to imitate her humble, meditative approach: to be less eager to overthrow what we do not like or do not understand and more ready to ponder, to think deeply about things in our hearts, to develop the art of meditation, to receive God on His own terms.

Bishop Jeremy Taylor, in a memorable passage, contrasts the inner spiritual devotion of our Lady with the busy, external action of St. Paul, Apostle and Missionary. Taylor captures the quiet piety and contemplative spirit of St. Mary in lovely phrases like "the internal actions of love" and "those graces which walk in

Oxford (M.S. Eng.th.e.51), cited in John Barnes, *XV Devotions of our Lady from Anglican Writers of the XVII Century* (The Society of St. Peter & St. Paul, 1973), p. 10.
[1]Athelstan Riley (1858-1945), "Ye watchers and ye holy ones," St. 2.
[2]Peter Toon, *Let Women Be Women*, p. 101.

a veil and silence."[1] Our Lord's Mother has much to teach us not only about quiet meditation but about ardent, soulful praise: "My soul doth magnify the Lord, and my spirit hath rejoiced in God my Saviour" (*Lk*. 1:46-47).

Renewed devotion to the Blessed Virgin Mary and deeper understanding of the feminine principles which she represents may help us to see the ordination of women in a proper light. For St. Mary, and for all of us, that true and acceptable point of view must be God's perspective, His divine order. And so, in faith and obedience, we must pray with our Lady: "Be it unto me according to thy word."

[1]*The Great Exemplar of Sanctity and Holy Life* (Life of Christ), Part I, *Ad* Section I.9. This passage is discussed admirably in A. M. Allchin, *The Joy of All Creation: An Anglican Meditation on the Place of Mary* (Dartman, Longman, & Todd, 1984), pp. 38-40.